Zen Macrobiotics

the art of rejuvenation and longevity

George Ohsawa
edited by Carl Ferré

D1257433

George Ohsawa Macrobiotic Foundation
Oroville, California

By George Ohsawa

The Art of Peace
The Essential Ohsawa
Gandhi, the Eternal Youth
Macrobiotics: An Invitation to
    Health and Happiness
Macrobiotics: The Way of Healing
The Order of the Universe
The Philosophy of Oriental Medicine
The Unique Principle
You Are All Sanpaku
Zen Macrobiotics

First (Mimeograph) Edition   1960
Second Edition   1962
Third (Oles) Edition   1965
Fourth Edition   1995

Back cover photo by Jacques deLangre

George Ohsawa Macrobiotic Foundation
P.O. Box 426, Oroville, California 95965
(916) 533-7702; fax (916) 533-7908

ISBN 0-918860-54-7

Preface to the Fourth Edition
by Carl Ferré

For the past thirty years many people have purchased, read, and been inspired by what has become known as "the little black book with the red circle on the cover." That third edition of *Zen Macrobiotics* by George Ohsawa was published by the Ohsawa Foundation in 1965 and was revised, edited, and annotated by Lou Oles and Shayne Oles Suehle. Thanks to their efforts *Zen Macrobiotics* contains some of Ohsawa's strongest and most direct suggestions for rejuvenation and longevity.

When we became aware that the seemingly endless supply of copies of the third edition had all been sold, we planned to reprint it in the same successful edition and format. However, Herman Aihara, founder and president of the George Ohsawa Macrobiotic Foundation, had a different idea. He showed me a copy of the original mimeograph edition that Ohsawa himself printed in New York City in 1960. Following this edition, Librarie J. Vrin published *Le Zen Macrobiotique* in French in 1961. Then there was a second English edition of *Zen Macrobiotics* between the mimeograph and Oles editions. Herman also wanted some misconceptions arising from the Oles edition corrected; so, we set to work on this new edition.

A careful reading of each edition showed that the Oles edition greatly improved the mimeograph edition and that there were two major differences. First, there were many sections added to the Oles edition from other Ohsawa writings. Since

3

they have been part of *Zen Macrobiotics* for so long, we decided to leave them in this edition. For those interested, the major parts added were the seventh condition of health added to chapter three, the entire chapter on yin-yang theory, most of the chapter on macrobiotic food for infants, and the entire section of appendices.

The other major difference is more significant. The mimeograph edition contained 240 recipes, of which only 50 appear in the Oles edition. There are many references in the Oles edition of *Zen Macrobiotics* to recipes in *Zen Cookery*. However, *Zen Cookery* never did contain all the recipes and the numbering system was not consistent with the numbers referred to in *Zen Macrobiotics*. Thus a lot of confusion has existed for many years.

It is with great joy that we announce the return of all the recipes from the original mimeograph edition to the new *Zen Macrobiotics*. These recipes will be very helpful in developing any cook's intuition but are not designed for those beginning macrobiotic cooking. Often there are no quantities of ingredients given, no cooking temperatures, no length of cooking times, etc. Those new to the macrobiotic style of food preparation should first study *Basic Macrobiotic Cooking* by Julia Ferré to learn the procedures of whole grain and fresh vegetable cookery. Many of the recipes in this edition of *Zen Macrobiotics* are spelled out more completely in *The First Macrobiotic Cookbook*, formerly *Zen Cookery*, and this book also makes a fine addition to any cook's library.

The main reason we decided to print the recipes as found in the mimeograph edition is that they show a side of Ohsawa that is often missed. The recipes themselves show a great variety of possibilities, both in preparation style and in ingredients used. Further, it shows Ohsawa's main goals and objectives were freedom, peace, and happiness. He taught that the best way to achieve these goals is through health and the easiest way to health is through eating the proper foods. Over the years much more emphasis has been placed on proper eating than on the true objectives of freedom and happiness.

The greatest misunderstanding from *Zen Macrobiotics* in all its editions has been generated by chapter five, Ten Healthful Ways of Eating and Drinking, in which Ohsawa clearly states the best way to health and happiness is by following diet number seven—grains only and as little as possible to drink. According to Herman Aihara, this advice would have been changed by Ohsawa once he understood Americans better. After all, Ohsawa came to the United States for the first time in 1959 and wrote and published *Zen Macrobiotics* specifically for Americans early in 1960. His dealings with the West were almost exclusively with the French. Asking the French to give up salads, desserts, vegetables, soups, etc. is like asking rabbits to give up sex.

Ohsawa told Herman that the French always cheated on their diets and that is why he recommended a number seven diet as the best. In this way he overstated the case so that they (the French) would eat more natural foods. Again according to Herman, Ohsawa had no idea that Americans had the will power to eat grains only for unusually long periods of time.

Today, the most common advice is to use diet number seven as a fast for a maximum of ten days, especially if recipes similar to those found in the Principal Food chapter are used. Noting that some of the dishes in that chapter contain vegetables, it is questionable whether diet number seven was ever intended to be grains only. And we can be fairly certain that brown rice only for extended periods of time was never Ohsawa's intention.

Liberty has been taken in changing book references to those available today and comments have been added in cases of changed macrobiotic opinion. These have been indicated by inserting bracketed material—[-ed.]. In this way advice that is no longer commonly accepted macrobiotic practice can be left for reference with today's opinion in brackets for your evaluation. Still, in the interest of space and time, minor changes made in the Oles edition that served only to improve the work have been left without annotation.

Whether this is your first reading of *Zen Macrobiotics* or your second or greater, we are certain you will benefit as countless others have by "the little black book with the red circle on the cover."

Preface to the Third Edition
by Shayne Oles Suehle

During his lifetime, George Ohsawa wrote more than 300 books and papers. This volume is considered the primer of the macrobiotic philosophy of Oriental medicine.

All of Ohsawa's basic thought is herein touched upon. But to those previously unacquainted with macrobiotics and its many implications in the realms of ancient and modernized Oriental philosophy and science, perhaps the main thrust of the macrobiotic way of living is its rediscovery of ancient basic truths regarding health.

The general path of Western medicine, from the Greeks and Egyptians on to the giant research centers of the present, has been in the direction of seeking cures for disease.

Oriental medicine, on the other hand, has for 5,000 years pursued a path whose goal has been the unity between the individual and "the way" — the way of nature herself, the eternal law governing all plants and creatures, the creation of an equilibrium between man and his biological destiny.

Western medicine has only recently begun turning its eyes toward this latter view, re-examining its own cure-oriented premise and gradually adapting its technology to ancient precepts of health. The amalgam of these two views is now known as "preventive medicine."

Zen Macrobiotics, therefore, should be considered as a guidebook whose aim is happiness → through health →

7

through nutrition.

In a period when the soil, water and very air of this planet is being bombarded with contamination through technology, no single individual is immune from the ravages of being alive in the twentieth century. Under such a violent assault upon each person's biological integrity, "preventive medicine" appears likely to be man's best defense of his "biological castle", his body.

Zen Macrobiotics, therefore, is presented to the reader as a last-best-hope. Health can be achieved. Health can be maintained. Man stands, precariously, between his dreams of a good world and his all-too-vulnerable mind and body.

It is the aim and hope of this book that each reader, by understanding its message, will find his own "way" to follow the dreams of his imagination through coming ever-closer to the biological dream of freedom from illness by preventing disease.

Foreword
Two Ways to Happiness

Happiness is the goal of everyone in this world. But, what is happiness in the Occident, or more particularly, in the United States?

Happiness was defined by Oriental sages some thousands of years ago as a state of being that is determined by five factors:

1. A joyfulness resulting from a healthy, productive and exciting longevity;

2. The freedom from worry about money;

3. An instinctive capacity to avoid the accidents and difficulties that could cause premature death;

4. A loving realization of the order that governs the infinite universe;

5. A deep comprehension of the fact that one must be last in order to become the first forever. This implies the abandonment of the goal of being the victor, the winner, or first-in-line in any situation since the attainment of this goal guarantees one's being last eventually. Everything changes in business, politics, science, marriage, in all of life — there is always a new winner. That which is the height of fashion today is out-of-date tomorrow. The man of humility, he who has no fear of being last, therefore, knows a contentment that is the essence of happiness.

Oriental philosophy — biological, physiological, social, economical and logical in its scope — teaches the practical way to achieve such happiness. It prohibits the explanation by any teacher of the deep significance of the structure of the infinite universe and its order. The student must discover this significance, the path to happiness, for himself. Accordingly, there are no theoretical discussions, only practical ones. Schools and professional education, are considered unnecessary, the makers of slaves. Further, the slave mentality is clearly seen as the cause of all misery and unhappiness. (It is interesting to note that the majority of great men have been autonomous — self-made.)

In this guidebook, I have avoided a complete explanation of the yin-yang philosophy of happiness, of the concept of supreme judgment and the keys to the kingdom of heaven for two reasons. Firstly, so many works have already been written on the subject,[1] and secondly, the intellectual, conceptual understanding of such philosophy is utterly useless if there is no practical result. To theorize is not enough; one must actually achieve a happy life that continually grows fuller.

The swimming of even the smallest fish cannot be mastered without first getting into the water. If you are interested in and excited by the Oriental philosophy that guarantees the five elements of happiness outlined above, please try the macrobiotic technique in this volume for a week or two. I can still recommend it after having taught it for more than forty-eight years; I am convinced that it is the fundamental way to happiness. The alternate way, via philosophical, intellectual, conceptual, theoretical study is difficult, tiresome, endless and disappointingly fruitless.

Above all, remember that this philosophy, that which I have called the Unique Principle is practical. It is not merely another one of the medical methods that pretends to restore bodily health while actually increasing the numbers of sickly, diseased people through endlessly new pharmaceutical products and surgical operations. It is simply a practical discipline of life that anyone can observe with great pleasure. It restores both the health and the harmony of soul, mind, and body that are essential for joyful living.

Preface to the First Edition
From Health to Peace

All the great religions of man were born in the Orient — the light from the East. Thanks to them, the people of that part of the world lived for thousands of years with relatively few cruel wars. (This included the Japanese, whose country had always been called the land of longevity and peace.)

Yet, everything changes in this ephemeral, floating, relative and limited world that we inhabit. With the importation of Occidental civilization, Asiatic and African countries that had been colonized gave up their traditional ways and naively and peacefully adopted the manner of the West.

Western civilization has since grown more powerful, war has progressively become more violent while modern science, which we admire very much, has emerged as the new religion of man.

May we hope that both this strikingly new, productive civilization and the ancient civilization of health, freedom, happiness and peace will become complementary — the two arms of oneness?

For forty-eight years my goal has been to accomplish just this, and at last I think I have found the way.

You in the Occident should study our five-thousand-year-old philosophy. With this dialectical, paradoxical, non-violent tool you will be able to solve not only scientific, social and medical problems, but you will discover the way to achieve happiness and freedom. Study and reach an understanding of our simple, practical and stimulating viewpoint. Remember, we imported everything from the West for more than one hundred years, sometimes voluntarily and sometimes not; it is now time for you to import this ageless, priceless treasure from the East.

First of all, learn about Eastern eating and drinking — macrobiotics, the structural basis for health and happiness.[2]

In Japan, for example, eating and drinking were once considered to be the most divine art of life. Whereas we, on the one hand, developed a method based on thought-out, well-established principles, Americans on the other hand, appear to be guided only by taste and pleasure in their food habits.

Macrobiotics is the fundamental way of eating and drinking in the Zen Buddhist monastery where it is called "Syozin Ryori," the cooking that develops the supreme judgment. This is consistent with the belief that physiology precedes and determines psychology. By contrast, what is customarily served in Chinese and Japanese restaurants in the United States appeals to the low, sensory judgment; it completely eclipses higher judgment. The true masters of Oriental cooking can prepare food according to macrobiotic principles that not only tastes delicious but also creates health and happiness.

You, too, can learn hundreds of ways to cook and eat, each one different from those usually found in restaurants, markets and home cooking, and each one designed to promote your well-being.

If the food industry in America were to adopt and industrialize macrobiotic food and drink, we might witness the first food revolution in the history of mankind and the first all-out war on human sickness and misery.

To My Readers

If you should decide to study our five-thousand-year-old philosophy in order to realize infinite freedom, eternal happiness
and absolute righteousness, understand that you must do this
on your own, independently, by and for yourself, as do all animals, birds, insects and fish. First of all, make up your mind to
conquer your sickness — not his or hers, but yours!

Learn the nature of your disease and its cause. If you are
only interested in the disappearance of symptoms, difficulties
or pain, you have no need to study this book. This unique philosophy does not deal with symptomatic medicine.

Assimilate and come to understand the Unique Principle
thoroughly; you must live it in your daily life. (The philosophy of Far Eastern medicine is quite sufficient — there is no
need to read and memorize thousands of very complicated
books.)

Observe the macrobiotic diet as it is explained. If you cannot find a specific treatment for the disease you are interested
in curing, apply one treatment or another or combine several
treatments described in Chapter 10 — according to the symptoms you have. Do this cautiously and systematically and you
will achieve success.

You yourself can be the creator of your own life, health
and happiness.

Contents

CHAPTER 1

Macrobiotics and Oriental Medical Philosophy

The way of health-to-happiness should be open to everyone; it should be practical as well as theoretical. Any theory, be it scientific, religious or philosophical, is useless if it is too difficult to understand or impractical for daily living. By the same token, any art, practice or technique is dangerous if it has no firm, theoretical foundation.

Macrobiotics is neither an empirical folk medicine nor a mystical, palliative, religious, scientific, spiritual, symptomatic technique. It is the biological and physiological application of Oriental philosophy and medicine, a dialectical conception of the infinite universe. This approach is five thousand years old and shows the way to happiness via health. It is very simple in practice. Anyone can adopt it in his daily life, anywhere, anytime, if he genuinely wants to be free of all physiological or mental difficulties.

It is because of the macrobiotic teaching of Lao-tse, Sun Tzu-wu, Confucius, Buddha, Nagarjuna, the Shintoists, and long before them, the sages who produced the great medical science of India, that millions of people in the Far East enjoyed happiness and freedom, culture and comparative peace for thousands of years. They, along with the ancient Greeks, knew that a sound, clear mind cannot exist in a tense, disturbed body.

Nevertheless, everything that has a beginning has an end. Today, all these teachings have become obsolete, pervaded by mysticism, professionalism and superstition. For this reason, I offer a new interpretation of the macrobiotic way of life. It is the prerequisite for an understanding of any philosophy of the Orient.

The Purpose of this Book

Why are there so many hospitals and sanatoriums, drugs and medicines, so many mental and physical illnesses in modern Western civilization? Why is there the need for so many prisons, the great numbers of police, the vast air, sea and land forces?

The answer is very simple. We are sick, physiologically and mentally. How can this be in the midst of such a highly developed society? Again the answer is a simple one. We are quite ignorant of the real cause of all suffering, unaware of its biological, moral, philosophical and psychological roots. Why? Because we are thus educated. Modern education does not foster the capacity in human beings for liberty, happiness and justice. On the contrary, it trains man to be professional. He is taught to be an irrational slave — cruel, simple-minded and attached to money.

Happiness or misery, health or sickness, freedom or slavery — all depend upon the manner in which we conduct our daily lives and activities. Our conduct is dictated by our judgment. It, in turn, is a result of our comprehension of the structure of the world and the infinite universe. Unfortunately, there is no school or university where we can learn to judge, think and understand with clarity and freedom. In France, for example, I have seen FREEDOM, EQUALITY, FRATERNITY in big letters everywhere, but never in reality.

Life is infinitely entertaining and wonderful. With the exception of man, all living things — birds, insects, fish, microbes, even parasites — live happily in nature: free, never employed, never obliged by others or by themselves. During the three years that I lived in the Indian and African jungles, I never once met a monkey, crocodile, serpent, ant or elephant that was unhappy, diseased or working for money. I found among these creatures of nature not one that was asthmatic, cancerous, diabetic, rheumatic or a victim of high or low blood pressure. All primitive people living among them were also relatively happy and healthy before the invasion by colonizers armed with guns, alcohol, chocolate and Christianity. The only principle of life for these primitives was this: "He who cannot enjoy life, must not eat."

I am the only and perhaps the "last angry man" of the colored race who wants to live the happy life of his ancestors. I want to re-establish a kingdom where "those who cannot enjoy life must not eat." (Epictetus has said that if one is unhappy, it is his own fault.[3]) Here, there is neither employer, employee, teacher, school, hospital, artificial medicine, police, prison, war nor enemy; there is no forced labor, no crime, no punishment. All are intimate friends, brothers, sisters, parents, children, wives or husbands; all are independent, autonomous.

I am not a revolutionist and have no desire to recreate a visible World Empire. My sole purpose in writing is to invite a few people to the invisible paradise that has been called "Erewhon" by Samuel Butler and "Wonderland" by Lewis Carroll. Admission is certain and free if they live macrobiotically and understand the philosophy of Oriental medicine.[4]

The Philosophy of the Far East

Once upon a time, there was a great, free man named Hou'i who discovered a curious stone key that opened the invisible door to the kingdom of heaven, "moni-kodo" in Japanese. (Just as erewhon is nowhere spelled backwards in English, so moni-kodo is doko-nimo, or Japanese for nowhere, spelled in reverse.) Hou'i lived on a high plateau in the heart of an aged continent that was extremely hot in the daytime and cold at night. He was without weapons, mechanical devices, clothing, shoes, shelter, money or drug stores. In spite of this, he enjoyed life with all his companions — the birds, fish, butterflies and prehistoric animals. He had no law or power to constrain him; there was no dictator, thief, journalist, doctor, telephone, passport, visa, inspector or taxation. Nothing bothered him.

Millions of years passed. Society was born, followed by civilization. Teachers appeared; education began. That is, professional teachers manufactured a facsimile of the curious stone key of Hou'i and set a high enough price on it to tempt everyone into wanting one of his own. This imitation has been selling well for thousands of years, right up to the present.

At this time, I would like to distribute the genuine key to the kingdom of freedom, happiness and justice. As opposed to the professional teacher, I enjoy my life without attachment to possessions or money, thus I can offer that key free of charge to all those who will trouble to take it.

In order to accomplish my mission, I speak in a special, child-like language that can easily be understood by those who merit free admission to that domain.

How can you be certain that you have understood my teaching? Very simple. He who understands it can re-establish his health, physiologically and psychologically: liberty, happiness and justice are his.

My interpretation of this kingdom is called "the philosophy of the Far East." It is difficult to comprehend for those who have been educated by professional teachers all their lives, not because of its theoretical complexity but because of its great simplicity. Yet for those who are not completely indoctrinated, it is easy to follow and practice. (I would be so very happy if even a handful of people could understand it fully.)

I present to you the key, in reality a guidebook, to the kingdom of heaven. It is my re-interpretation of the Far Eastern philosophy that has been completely falsified, mutilated and transformed by professional learned men and saints over the years. Teachers in modern civilization unfortunately appear likely to continue this desecration.

My new version of the old is built on the firm foundation of Far-Eastern medicine, a physiological and biological application of prehistoric philosophy. All five great religions of man spring from the same rich source. Here can be found the reason why Jesus was so miraculously successful as a healer of both physical and mental disease.

The medicine that can cure only physical disease is either a bad magician or a Satan who makes us more unhappy than we were before we encountered him. Mental agony and anxiety are the real Hell, unreachable by rocket and unseen by an electron microscope. Such illness is characteristic of the mentality of those who are ignorant of the structure of the universe and its laws, for to attempt the cure of diseases of the body while neglecting those of the mind is to attempt the impossible.

I am deeply convinced of the miraculous effectiveness of our philosophy-medicine. Because of it, I was able to rid myself of tuberculosis and other so-called incurable ailments after having had the good fortune to be given up by doctors before I was twenty. Since then, I have seen thousands of amazing cures throughout Africa, Asia, and Europe. Poor, desperate people who have applied this method for themselves have recovered their health. Like birds in the sky, fish in the sea and animals on the land, they have found their freedom.

Ten years ago, I left my native Japan with the sole idea in mind that I would visit every country in the world to find a handful of friends who might understand and adopt our way. I was seeking those who would realize that it might enable them to re-establish the invisible kingdom of holiness, wholesomeness and health on this planet.

Our philosophy-medicine is paradoxical, dialectical, easy even for children to learn and most practical. This treatment is not one whose prime objective is to destroy symptoms at any price through the use of chemical, physical or moral violence. It is a method that guarantees more than just a medical cure (simple elimination of symptoms) and the control of physiological health; it promises peace of soul, liberty and justice within one's lifetime. All this without any mechanical devices. It is more revolutionary than atomic energy or the hydrogen bomb. It upsets all values, all philosophies, all modern techniques.

The theory is simple: there is only one principle to understand, the same one that Toynbee recognized at the conclusion of his long research into history: yin-yang.[5] The yin-yang dialectical principles — a logical, cosmological foundation for existence, a universal compass, the heart of a world conception — can be applied throughout our daily life, on every level, whether family, marital, social or political.[6]

After having taught this method for forty-eight years, I am

convinced of its great value. Yet, there is still the chance that I may be wrong. Otherwise, why in all these years have I been able to find so few Western doctors or philosophers who can understand the unity of philosophy and medicine that was taken for granted in the East in years gone by?

CHAPTER 2

What is My Therapy?

According to Far Eastern medicine as I understand it, there need be no therapeutics or remedies because the mother of all life in the universe, nature herself, is the greatest healer. All disease, unhappiness, crime and punishment result from behavior that violates the order of the universe.

The cure is, therefore, infinitely simple! Merely stop violating that order and allow nature to do her miraculous work.

All disease can be cured completely in ten days, according to our philosophical conception of the world and of the structure of the universe. All disease is located in or fed by our blood. Since we decompose one-tenth of that blood every second, it should be entirely transformed and completely renewed in ten days if we follow a natural way of eating and drinking. What is natural is determined by the consideration of both the innate biological needs of the human organism and the needs that are superimposed by environmental conditions such as weather, altitude, type of activity and time of year.

Although the theory and its logic are quite understandable, the technique of its application is delicate and can be very complex. In keeping with the traditional Oriental belief that no theory without a practical technique is useful and that no technique without an uncomplicated, clear theory is safe, my therapy is very simple:

1. natural food
2. no medicine
3. no surgery
4. no inactivity

Granted, it is very difficult to find natural food and drink today. Yet, if you have understood the unique principle of all Eastern philosophy and science (the structure of the universe and its order), nothing can discourage you. You will succeed.

Again, theory is simple in our ages-old philosophy. But its application in our daily lives can be as complicated as our modern kitchens, agriculture and industry have become. Everything depends upon your understanding and accuracy.[7]

Unhappiness, Illness and Crime

The failure and decay of world empires and their civilizations have come from within themselves, as Toynbee realized.[8] Likewise, the unhappiness, disease and crime of man come from within himself. His own blindness to life and ignorance of the structure of the universe are the root of all his suffering, for man is born in the center of heavenly happiness as the prince or princess of creation.

Incurable Disease in Man

Incurable disease in man is a misnomer and a product of the imagination. I have seen thousands of incurable diseases such as asthma, diabetes, epilepsy, leprosy and paralyses of all kinds cured by dialectical macrobiotics in ten days or a few weeks. I am convinced that there is no incurable disease in all the world if we apply this method correctly.

Three Categories of Cure

According to our theory, there are three categories of cure:

1. Symptomatic: Elimination and destruction of symptoms by symptomatic methods — palliative, physical, violent cure. This is symptomatic, animal or mechanical medicine.

2. Educational: Improvement of judgment to enable man to establish and maintain personal control of his physical health. This is the medicine of man.

3. Creative, Spiritual: A life without fear or anxiety, a life of freedom, happiness and justice — the realization of self. This is the medicine of the mind, the body and the soul.

If you are not certain that you want the third category of cure, by and for yourself and at any price, you have no need to study this book. You can find a temporary cure in the first category through popular, orthodox or folk medicine; one in the second category can be achieved through some spiritual or psychological method. The third category, however, is the everlasting structure that rises above the failures of the other two.

What We Must Not Cure

No disease is incurable for God, Creator of this infinite universe — the kingdom of freedom, happiness and justice. Nevertheless, there are some sick people who cannot be cured, and who cannot be taught to cure themselves. They are the arrogant ones who do not wish to know first of all the structure of the infinite universe and its unique principle (the kingdom of heaven and its justice). They do not realize that without this knowledge they cannot have the faith that orders the mountain to enter the sea.

If you do not have the will to live most simply and happily, you must not and cannot be cured. Vivere parvo.[9]

Sick people incessantly express the wish for a cure; they claim to have the will to rid themselves of disease at any cost. Will of this variety is merely a desire to escape from the status quo — defeatism. It reveals an unwillingness to accept the eternal order in life, the order that oscillates between difficulty and pleasure. To exist in a static state that includes only the one and not the other is impossible: We must continually re-create our own happiness by recognizing and curing disease at every instant of our lives.

Many a man wishes to be cured by others or by some mechanical device, all the while by-passing his own involvement and personal responsibility, the cause of his disease: Mea culpa . . . my crime. People of this sort are descendants of the race of vipers. They do not deserve a complete cure or the kingdom of heaven. They must not and in fact, cannot be cured.

The will, by contrast, is unique and works in quite a different manner. The will to live seeks and finds, first of all, the beginning cause of all unhappiness, all disease, all injustice in the world and then proceeds to eliminate it without using violent, artificial means. It conquers through methods that are in accord with the structure of the infinite universe, naturally and peacefully.

The drive to cure only symptoms or to have control of one's health without accepting responsibility is comparable to the notion on the part of an individual that he can step in front of a moving train and not be struck down. It is simple exclusiveness and egoism; it eclipses and denies will, the order in the infinite universe.

Satori

Satori, for the Oriental, is the tangible and logical conviction that he has arrived, body and soul in the kingdom of freedom, happiness and justice.

If your way to satori seems interminably long, your orientation cannot be right. Your slow progress is undoubtedly a result of the viewpoint originally expressed by men of science like Du Bois Reymond and Henri Poincare: "Ignoramus, ignorabimus — we do not know, we shall never know." This, in essence, is the position of the scientific and philosophical research that dominates the world today. Yet, what science feels can never be known was known thousands of years ago in the Orient. To find satori, you need but change your orientation: "Ignoramus → satori — we humbly admit that we do not know anything but we believe that it is possible to know; let us meditate (think) and study deeply, then we will know all." (Each macrobiotic center is called "Centre Ignoramus" for this reason.)

There is nothing occult or mystical about the concept of satori. To attain it, study our philosophy (the very foundation of all religions) so that you can understand the marvelous structure of the infinite universe and its justice. Then, practice the technique called macrobiotics, daily and strictly.

A good driver or navigator knows the construction, mechanism, value and function of his vehicle and the laws of energy. Similarly, you are obligated to know and be the doctor of your own body. All birds, fish and animals in Nature are good drivers and navigators. Even the microbe is his own doctor and so never needs a hospital or a drug store. The drug store is the symbol or barometer of the ignorance of a population that is oblivious to mea culpa.

Courage, Honesty, Justice

He who is applauded for being a courageous man does not know courage. He is so completely involved in his courageous action that he has no time to contemplate what he does. That is, he does not know what it is in the sense that we, as observers of his action, know it. Likewise, he who is one hundred percent honest does not know what honesty is nor does he who is righteous know righteousness. Further, the healthy person knows not health. They are all humble. Knowledge is the identification card of the limited, relative illusory world, not of the infinite kingdom of heaven.

If you are sure of your ability, quality, power, knowledge or fortune, you are the prisoner of this limited world. If you claim to know courage, honesty, justice, patience or health, you have no modesty and in reality you are a stranger to all of them.

Here is the core of the matter: courage, honesty, justice, happiness and freedom cannot be given to one person by another. You must realize them by yourself and for yourself. If they depend upon others or upon certain conditions, they are all borrowed and not truly your own.

If someone guarantees your freedom, your freedom is your debt. The greater such freedom, the greater your debt.

Happiness, freedom and justice must be infinite, unconditional, unlimited. If you seek them from others or if they are dependent on the conditions of your society, your debt is endless. Your life is that of a slave.

Tolerance

If you have to learn to be tolerant, you reveal your understanding is limited. There is nothing intolerable in this world. All things are tolerable.

The whole of nature (birds, bees, animals, fish and every truly free human being) accepts all with great pleasure: bad weather like good, death like life, difficulty like joyfulness. There is neither protest, objection nor complaint for everything is in equilibrium.

If you find the most insignificant thing to be intolerable, you yourself are intolerable and exclusive. Since it is impossible for you to destroy or expel all the things in this world to which you might object, your existence is of necessity a frustrated one, a living hell.

If tolerance is your slogan, you are an intolerant person since all such slogans are an involuntary confession of your true nature. Medicine, for example, does not actually cure disease; it merely wages war on symptoms while completely ignoring first causes. As a consequence, patients and doctors both die of one disease or another, despite endless campaigns to eradicate germs, microbes and viruses. This is a striking case of intolerance, intolerance of the existence of God's creatures.

Absolute justice is another name for the irrevocable order in the universe. It includes good and bad, right and wrong. These opposites are antagonistic in that they are opposite, yet they are complementary because they do and must exist side by side in our world; they are the front and back of the same coin. To exterminate one for the sake of the other is impossible; even to attempt this extermination is the height of ignorance — intolerance. The judge with no understanding of absolute justice, therefore, cannot possibly hand down a valid decision.

Further, law enforcement by the police, as we well know, can never cure society of the disease of crime; it only battles symptoms unsuccessfully through the apprehension and punishment of the criminal. It substitutes intolerance of the symptom (in this case the criminal) for the deep study of the primary cause of the disease (crime) and its complete cure.

He who accepts everything with great pleasure has no need to know the meaning of tolerance.

CHAPTER 3

The Seven Main Conditions of Health and Happiness

Before observing my dietetic directions, it would be wise for you to evaluate the state of your health in accordance with the seven conditions that follow.

The first three conditions are physiological; if you satisfy them all, you score fifteen points or five points for each. The fourth, fifth and sixth, psychological in nature, are valued at ten points each. The seventh and most important condition of all is worth fifty-five points. In all, there are a total of one hundred points.

Those who score more than forty points at first are in relatively good health. Should you total sixty points in three months, it will be a great success for you.

Be sure to do this self-consultation before you try the macrobiotic diet and again at the beginning of each month following. In this way, you will be able to check your progress and the rigor of your application.

Try this test on your friends. You will be surprised to find that some of them are actually in very poor health although their outward appearance may be quite good.

Read and re-read this guidebook to the philosophy of the Far East. Each time you will find deeper meaning in it.

1. NO FATIGUE:

You should not feel fatigued. If you catch cold, your organism has been tired for many years. Even one cold in ten years is a bad sign for there is no bird or insect that ever catches cold, even in cold countries and cold weather. The root of your disease is therefore very deep. If you are prone to saying, "It is too difficult," "It is impossible," or "I am not prepared for such a thing," you reveal the extent of your problem.

If you are really healthy, you can overpower and chase away difficulties one after the other as a dog chases a rabbit. If you avoid ever larger difficulties, however, you are a defeatist.

We must be adventurers in life since today unceasingly advances into tomorrow, the unknown. The bigger the difficulty, the bigger the pleasure. This attitude is the sign of freedom from fatigue.

Fatigue is the real foundation of all diseases. You can cure it without any medicine if you understand and practice the macrobiotic way to longevity and rejuvenation.

2. GOOD APPETITE:

If you cannot take the simplest food with joy, pleasure and deep gratitude to God the Creator, your appetite is poor. If you find simple whole-grain bread or cooked whole brown rice very appetizing, you have a good appetite and a healthy strong stomach. A good appetite for food and sex is health itself.

Sexual appetite and joyful satisfaction are an essential condition of happiness. If a man or woman has no appetite for sex and experiences no pleasure, he or she is estranged from the dialectical law of life, yin-yang. Violation of this law through ignorance can only lead to sickness and insanity.

All those who are vexed and angry, inside or out, are Puritans: they shrink from sexuality, are impotent and can never enter the kingdom of heaven.

3. DEEP AND GOOD SLEEP:

If you dream or speak in your sleep, your sleep is not deep and good. Your sleep is healthy if four to six hours of it satisfies you entirely. If you cannot get profound sleep within three or four minutes after putting your head on the pillow, under any circumstance, at any time, your mind is not free from some fear. Your sleep has been imperfect if you cannot awaken spontaneously at an hour pre-determined by you before retiring.

4. GOOD MEMORY:

Memory is the single most important factor in our lives, the foundation of our personality, the compass of our life. Without a strong memory, without a storehouse of varied memories, we are nothing but cybernetic machines.[10] For example, very young children, fascinated by fire and unable to resist the impulse to touch it, eventually get burned. The memory of this experience usually causes them to handle fire with care for the rest of their lives. Therefore, human behavior, if it is not to end in misfortune, depends on sound judgment. Sound judgment, in turn, depends on remembered experience.

Since the capacity to remember increases with age, it is possible to improve our memory infinitely, even to the extent of not forgetting anything that we see or hear. We can thus avoid the miserable feeling that comes from not remembering those who have been kind to us.

We should emulate the good Yogi and the Buddhist or Christian saint whose infinite memory enabled them to visualize their anterior [preceding] life.

Through our macrobiotic directions, we can re-establish and infinitely strengthen this faculty. A striking example of this is the diabetic whose lost memory can be restored very rapidly through macrobiotics. Happily, this is true not only for the diabetic: even an idiot, imbecile or neurasthenic can be amazingly successful in regaining his original retentive power.

In a city in France there is a philosopher, Mrs. L. Along with her husband and four children, she began the macrobiotic way of eating and drinking three years ago to strengthen her memory and general physical condition. To her delight, her eldest daughter, age 14, reached the head of her class.

5. GOOD HUMOR:

A man of good health is free from anger, fear or suffering and is cheerful and pleasant under all circumstances. The more difficulties and enemies he has, the more happy, brave and enthusiastic he becomes.

Your appearance, voice, behavior and even your criticism should distribute deep gratitude and thankfulness to all those who are in your presence. All your words should be expressive of a deep gratitude, like the singing of birds and insects or the poems of Tagore. The stars, the sun, the mountains, rivers and seas are all ours. How can we exist without being happy? We should be full of delight like a boy who has just received a magnificent present. If we are not, we lack good health and are particularly deficient in this fifth condition, good humor. The healthy person never gets angry!

How many intimate friends have you? A large number and variety of them indicates a profoundly deep comprehension of the universe. Parents, brothers and sisters are not friends, as such. A friend is he who you like, admire and respect; he who likes and admires you; he who helps you to realize your fondest dreams at all costs, forever, without being asked.

How many dear friends have you? If the number is few, you are a very exclusive person or a sad delinquent without enough good humor to make others happy. If, however, you have more than two billion intimate friends, you can say that you are a friend of all mankind. It is not sufficient if your intimate friends include only human beings, living or dead. You will have to love and admire all beings and things, including grains of sand, drops of water and blades of grass. Dr. S. Margine said, "Each time I am in the presence of the work of nature, I enjoy and admire the simplicity of her means."[11] Will Rogers has said, "I never met a man I didn't like."[12]

If you cannot make your wife or children into intimate friends, you are very sick. If you are not cheerful under any circumstances, you are a blind man who sees neither this limited world of relativity nor the infinite, absolute universe, both full of marvels. If you have any complaint, be it mental, moral, physiological or social, shut yourself in a private room like the shellfish and speak out your sorrow to yourself alone.

If you have few intimate and loyal friends, it would be wise to observe these directions: take a small spoonful of gomashio (sesame seeds ground with salt) to neutralize the acidity of your blood. The value of this advice can be illustrated by a small experiment with your children. Stop giving them the sugar, honey and chocolate candy that acidify their blood: an unhappy, yin child will become yang and joyful in a week or two.[13]

Sesame seeds and salt in combination (four portions of grilled sesame seed powder with one portion of sea salt) destroy the bad effect of sugar on the whole human organism, and particularly on the nervous and cerebral systems. Each grain of salt is covered with the oil of crushed sesame seeds and causes no thirst. It meanwhile penetrates the bloodstream and reduces the over-acidity of the blood to normal.

Remember, acidity in excess and death are one and the same!

Rarely do we encounter men or women of agreeable temperament. The vast majority of them do not know how to attain good humor, yet they are not to be blamed: they are sick. They know neither what nor how to eat or drink. If you are truly conscious of the wonderful structure of the universe, you should be full of infinite joy and gratitude. And you cannot help but share this joy and gratitude with others. Give good humor, a smile, an agreeable voice and the simple words, "thank you," under all circumstances and as often as you can.

In the Occident one says, "Give and take;" in the East we say, "Give, give and give, infinitely." You lose nothing at all by imitating us for you have received life itself — the whole universe — without paying. You are the unique son or daughter of the infinite universe; it creates, animates, destroys and reproduces everything necessary for you. If you know this, everything will come to you in abundance.

If you are afraid of losing your money; or your property through the practice of the principle of "Give, give and give," you are sick and unhappy, a victim of oblivion. You have entirely forgotten the origin of your fortune and life, the infinite universe; your supreme judgment is partially or totally eclipsed; you are unable to see the grand order of the infinite universe. Blindness of judgment is more dreadful and desperate than blindness of sight. You must cure it as soon as possible, so that you may enjoy this splendid order of the infinite universe.

If you give someone a small or large part of your fortune, do not consider it to be an application of our Oriental principle, "Give, give, and give, infinitely." You are applying here the idea of "give and take," the basic Occidental economic principle used as a device to justify the violent colonization and exploitation of all colored people. The many so-called social workers, probably the worst offenders in the Occident, give only the fruits of exploitation and begging. To give that which you have received from others is not at all a sacrifice. We are reminded of Ali Baba who gave only that which he had originally stolen from forty thieves.

Oriental giving, by contrast, is sacrifice, an expression of infinite gratitude and the realization of self-liberation, of freedom from all debt. To sacrifice means to give the biggest and best thing we have. Sacrifice is an offering to the eternal love, infinite liberty and absolute justice of life. Real sacrifice is the act of joyfully giving our life or giving the omniscient, omnipotent and omnipresent principle of life. It is satori — self-liberation. Mother Earth gives herself to feed the grass, infinitely. The grass gives itself to feed animals, infinitely. The animals give life to make this world joyful, happy and interesting, year in and year out. But the human being kills and destroys everything. Why does man not give himself for others? In creation, one dies and is transformed into new life. Man, in his turn, should give of himself to realize the most splendid miracle of creation: infinite freedom, eternal happiness and absolute justice. Those who cannot understand this are either slaves, sick men or mad.

If you are cheerful, beloved by all people everywhere, always giving to others of the biggest and best thing in this world, you will become the happiest of all — the one in a million able to express the greatest joy.

By observing our macrobiotic directions, you can achieve all this. You can actually find the new horizons called "Shangri-La" and "Erewhon" of which man has merely dreamed for more than 300,000 years.[14]

Macrobiotic medicine is in reality a kind of Aladdin's lamp, a Flying Carpet with which you can realize your fondest dreams. But to achieve this, you must first of all re-establish your health and gain at least sixty points as outlined in the Seven Main Conditions of Health.

6. CLARITY IN THINKING AND DOING:

Those people in good health should have the ability to think, judge and do with promptness and clarity: promptness is the expression of Freedom. Those who are prompt, quick, precise and ready to answer any challenge or necessity are healthy.

They distinguish themselves by their ability to establish order everywhere. This orderliness can be observed throughout the animal and vegetable kingdoms. Beauty of action or form is an expression of the comprehension of the order of the infinite universe. Health and happiness, wholesomeness and holiness are also expressions of the order translated into our daily lives. Divinity, eternity, health and life are one.

7. THE MOOD OF JUSTICE:

Those persons with a complete understanding of justice have reached satori, for justice = health = supreme judgment = oneness = infinity = satori. They know the philosophy of the Far East in all its profundity and have earned a full one hundred points in our self-evaluation test.

If, however, you have not reached this level, you can still earn fifty-five points, provided that justice is not merely a concept or idea about which you only dream. If you are actively involved in coming to know what it represents, if every day brings you closer to a full understanding of the order of nature, if your intention or goal is to grasp the deepest meaning of the philosophy of the Far East, you have caught the mood of justice. Your growing comprehension will lead to self-realization and merits fifty-five points.

The mood of justice is revealed by your tendency to live in accordance with the natural order of the universe, by your inclination to recognize yin and yang in every phenomenon, be it physical, mental or spiritual, on every level of daily life such as eating, drinking, thinking, judging, doing, speaking, buying, selling, reading, walking and working.

In other words, you should live the biological law: From one grain, ten thousand grains. All vegetables and animals return ten thousand times more than they receive. One grain is given to the earth; the earth gives back ten thousand grains. One silkworm fed by man gives hundreds of thousands of eggs plus ten thousand yards of silk yarn. Some female fish give billions of eggs. Such is the natural biological law.

If your parents have given you life and have fed you to the age of ten, take care of them infinitely, ten times ten thousand. When they are gone, help the parents of others directly through your own action or indirectly through other means. This is the Oriental concept of "On" that has been completely misunderstood in the West. It is not merely the discharge of a debt. It is far more than that. On is joyfulness in distributing infinite freedom and eternal happiness; it is justice or the absolute joy of life.

Justice, at first glance, would appear to have no connection whatever with diet. It might seem that diet, a practicality, has been replaced by a useless abstraction similar to those that have plagued other philosophies for thousands of years. This is misleading for diet is justice and justice is diet; they are one.

To follow the macrobiotic way is to come to know justice; by the same token, to know justice is to follow the macrobiotic way, the order of nature or life itself.

Since nature has provided us with foods that are proper for our bodies, we can achieve health by recognizing and using them. This is macrobiotics, the materialization of the order of nature in our eating and drinking. If we live according to this order, health can result; if we are ignorant of it, unhappiness and disease are more likely to follow. This is simple, clear and practical. It is true justice.

*   *   *   *   *

The seven conditions outlined above cannot be realized without observing the macrobiotic directions absolutely. Observing these directions is simple and direct. You can be the creator of your own life, health and happiness without relying on others; you can be independent and free. Physical, mental and moral disease can be cured with macrobiotics, the product of a wisdom that is five thousand years old.

Do you have a more modern, simple or direct method?

I do not know of one, although my judgment may be poor and there may actually be a better way. If there is, please tell me about it. I am ready to follow you and discard the biological, physiological and cosmological way of health to peace that I have pursued joyfully for forty-eight years.

CHAPTER 4

If You Have Faith, Nothing Shall Be Impossible to You

Philosophy in the Orient is the art of teaching the constitution of the infinite universe, the kingdom of heaven.[15] Its sole purpose is to help man to understand this constitution (or order) so that he can realize his freedom, happiness and health for himself and by himself. Since this theory is not only dialectical but also paradoxical and deep, I have simplified it so that it can be understood by everyone.

The conception of the world and life, the constitution of the infinite universe, is translated first of all biologically and then physiologically. This is the firm foundation of all religions of the Orient. That is why there are more or less strict dietetic principles in all religions. Without living by these principles, one cannot understand or gain strength from one's religion and its teachings, a fact largely ignored by Western theologians.

In Buddhism, and particularly Zen Buddhism, there are strict dietetic principles to be observed. Yet, of the many books being published today in the West on Zen Buddhism and Indian philosophy, not one gives a full explanation of the importance and superiority of their biological and physiological basis. It is not surprising, therefore, that the philosophy of Vedanta, Taoism and Buddhism cannot be fully understood in

the West. If religions as a whole have lost their authority
through the centuries, it is because of the neglect or ignorance
of this same foundation. Accordingly, peace, freedom, health
and happiness are vanishing all over the world. Jesus said:

> If ye have faith as a grain of mustard seed,
> . . . ye shall say unto this mountain,
> "Remove hence to yonder place,"
> and it shall remove;
> and nothing shall be impossible unto you.
> —Matthew 27:20-21

If you have faith, nothing shall be impossible to you. If
something is impossible to you, you have not as much faith as
a grain of mustard seed. Crimes, hostility, poverty, wars and
especially so-called incurable illness are all the end result of a
lack of faith.

Happiness or unhappiness depends upon our behavior
which is in turn controlled by our judgment. Faith is the solid
foundation upon which judgment rises.

We must not confuse that type of judgment that is based
on faith with the variety that is not. The judgment that fails is
the latter. If your judgment fails, you are one who has not
even as much faith as a grain of mustard seed. Faith is judgment in infinity. If you do not know the order of the infinite
universe, you have no faith. If you have confidence only in
man-made contrivances such as laws, power, knowledge, science, money, drugs and medicines, you have faith only in relativity, not in infinity. Since all relative judgment is transitory
and of little value, you should learn the structure of infinity,
the eternal Creator.

This is why I have spent forty-eight years as an interpreter
of the philosophy of the Orient and why I wrote this guide-

book. It is a passport to the kingdom of health, freedom and happiness, where every being is his own master, free and healthy, never salaried, never dependent. Birds, fish, insects and microbes along with all herbs and trees live there in complete satisfaction without knowing the fear of sickness, old age or death. I shall be very happy if you can use this passport even for only ten days. If you decide to be happy, free, healthy and independent through observing the directions of our philosophy, contact me anytime and anywhere via the telephone called "Faith."

In the kingdom of life, one must learn everything for himself and by himself. There is no school or university because the infinite universe itself is the eternal school; there is no teacher because one can learn from everything and everyone, day and night. A strong, cruel enemy is particularly valuable; without him, one becomes idle, weak and stupid.

This guidebook to living is more than sufficient because the Oriental teacher of the Grand School teaches by asking questions: he rarely answers any of them so as to strengthen the student's ability to judge for himself. In the Grand School of Happiness and Freedom, learning comes only through practice. Theory must be imagined and invented through intuition and thinking. It is no wonder, therefore, that before coming to the West I had never before written a book that answered so many questions, not a single volume of this type among the more than three hundred writings I had published in Japanese.

You Should Have Infinite Freedom

If man is superior to all other animals, he should be able to cure himself more effectively than they can. The man who cannot cure himself, who cannot achieve his own freedom, happiness and absolute justice by and for himself, without being helped by others or by mechanical devices, is destined to be exploited and devoured, to feed worms and microbes. He has no need to go to hell after death for his existence is already a living hell.

The teachings of all great religions insist upon the importance of correct eating and drinking. The ancient Indian *Code of Manu* shows us a very practical physiological and biological way to establish happiness and peace on earth. It is truly amazing. Nevertheless, this wisdom is not put to use; it has been forgotten.

Everyone is born happy. If an individual does not continue to be happy, it is his own fault: through ignorance, he has violated the order of the universe.

If you wish to live a happy, interesting, amusing, joyful and long life, you should strengthen your comprehension and unveil your supreme judgment by taking natural, normal, righteous food. This method has been taught by all free men (the saints of the Orient) in the *Bible*, the *Canon of the Yellow Emperor*, the *I-Ching*, the *Tao-te-Ching*, the *Bhagavad-Gita* and the *Charak Samhita*.

Further, if there is even one person or thing in this world that you cannot like, you can never be happy. If you are unhappy, you are physiologically or psychologically sick. You must cure yourself without depending on others or on any device. Otherwise, your cure is incomplete, for you have lost your independence and your freedom.

Your happiness, freedom, justice, health and joyfulness must be completely yours. Health or freedom given by others is a debt that must be paid sooner or later if you are not to remain a slave or a thief.

Those who never say, "Thank you," those who often say

"Thank you," but never pay what they owe, those who think that they have paid all they owe by saying only, "Thank you" or "Thank you very much," are unhappy. They are more undesirable and detestable than a bandit. They suffer unto the last moment of their lives because their existence is a continuity of debts.

In truth, you cannot pay all that you owe in this life, because you have nothing but what you owe. You will be freed from debt if you distribute infinite joyfulness and thankfulness to everyone you meet throughout your life. This amounts to a real understanding of the structure of the infinite universe and its justice. The earth gives back ten thousand grains in return for each grain she has received. "One grain, ten thousand grains" is the biological law of this world. He who violates this law cannot live happily. If you cannot live by this law, you are most unfortunate, a man punished and confined in the prison called "Sickness, Misery or Difficulties."

You Must Be Your Own Doctor

Macrobiotics, the medicine of longevity and rejuvenation, is very simple, extraordinarily practical and economical. One can apply it at any time, on any level of life and under any circumstance. It is more educational than curative and depends entirely on your comprehension and will. It is in truth the study of the way to satori — realization of self and liberation — and you must achieve it yourself.

The many books written for this purpose over the ages are, generally speaking, conceptual, not practical. They are very beautiful to read and recite but very difficult to live by in daily life. By contrast, the art of longevity and rejuvenation, macrobiotics, is practical. You can discover this for yourself by complete and strict observance of its fundamental directions for only ten days.

This volume stresses the importance of correct eating and drinking. Should you desire to deepen your understanding of the philosophy on which macrobiotics is based, read *The Philosophy of Oriental Medicine*.[16]

CHAPTER 5

Ten Healthful Ways
of Eating and Drinking

There are ten ways of eating and drinking by which you can establish a healthy and happy life. The objective is to maintain a good balance of yin and yang in accordance with our cosmological, biological and physiological philosophy. Even without understanding the theory, however, you can follow any one of the ten ways of health to happiness by observing the following macrobiotic directions very carefully.

Ten Ways to Health and Happiness

diet no.	cereals	vegetable nitsuke	soup	animal	salads fruits	dessert	beverages
7	100%						see text
6	90%	10%					page 53
5	80%	20%					
4	70%	20%	10%				
3	60%	30%	10%				
2	50%	30%	10%	10%			
1	40%	30%	10%	20%			
-1	30%	30%	10%	20%	10%		
-2	20%	30%	10%	25%	10%	5%	
-3	10%	30%	10%	30%	15%	5%	

If you substitute fruits and salads for all animal food (Diets No. 2 through No. -3), you can be a vegetarian. If you find, however, that you still cannot achieve the state of well-being that you desire, try a higher way. The highest, Diet No. 7, is the easiest, simplest, and wisest. The lower the diet number, the more difficult. Try the easiest and simplest way for ten days, observing the following directions:

1. No industrialized food or drink such as sugar, soft drinks, dyed food, non-fertilized eggs,[17] canned or bottled food.[18]

2. For all cooking, see Chapters 6, 7, and 8, also *The First Macrobiotic Cookbook*, companion volume to this one.

3. Do not take any fruits and vegetables that are artificially produced with chemical fertilizers and/or insecticides.

4. Do not take any food that comes from a long distance since it requires preservatives that are very harmful.

5. Do not use any vegetable out of season.

6. Absolutely avoid the most yin vegetables: potatoes, tomatoes, and eggplant.

7. Take no spices or chemical seasoning (all commercial Japanese soy sauce and miso included). Exceptions: natural sea salt and macrobiotic-quality soy sauce and miso may be used.

8. Coffee is prohibited. Do not use tea containing carcinogen dyes. This includes most varieties that are available commercially. Japanese bancha tea and Chinese natural tea (undyed) are permitted.

9. Practically all animal food such as chicken, pork, beef, butter, cheese and milk, is chemically produced or treated. Avoid these. Most wild birds, fresh fish and shellfish, by contrast, are free from chemicals. They may be used occasionally.

10. Yeast, as defined in the *Oxford English Dictionary*, is a

yellowish substance that is produced as froth or sediment during the alcoholic fermentation of malt worts and other saccharine fluids. Since yeast, therefore, is sugar-based, those foods that contain it are to be eaten in small quantities.

11. Baked goods that contain baking soda are not used. The soda promotes rapid-rising and expansion in a dough mixture. As such, it is too yin to be part of a balanced, healthful diet.

With the improvement in your health and happiness that results from your growing comprehension of the Unique Principle, yin-yang, try lower ways in the schedule, slowly and carefully. That is, if you are very curious or adventurous. Otherwise, you can continue any way higher than No. 3 for as long as you like without any danger. If you are not getting better, try Diet No. 7 for one or two weeks or even months. (From time to time, you can measure your health and happiness by means of the self-consultation that utilizes the Seven Main Conditions of Health and Happiness starting on page 34.)

[WARNING: Because of unsatisfactory results over the years by some people using Diet No. 7 fanatically for long periods of time, current macrobiotic practice is to use Diet No. 7 as a ten-day fast only and to use lower numbers as guidelines for daily macrobiotic eating. One should remember that Ohsawa's main message is for each person to develop his or her judgment in order to gain complete freedom from following any diet prescribed by others, including Ohsawa himself. The diets printed here are to be used in the beginning of macrobiotic practice only until one's judgment and understanding has deepened to the point that they can eat whatever they want whenever they want without fear or ill effect. -ed.]

Chewing

You must chew every mouthful of food at least fifty times. If you wish to assimilate the macrobiotic philosophy as quickly as possible, chew each mouthful one hundred to one hundred and fifty times. I know of a Japanese girl who chewed a piece of onion thirteen hundred times.

"You must chew your drink and drink your foods," said Gandhi. The most tasteful morsel becomes more so if chewed well. Try chewing beef carefully, you will very rapidly find it to be tasteless.The foods that are good and necessary for your body become so delectable that you will not give them up until the end of your life.

Less Liquids

Learning to drink less is very much more difficult than learning to eat wisely and simply. But, it is very necessary. Seventy-five percent of our body weight is made up of water. Cooked rice, for example, contains sixty to seventy per cent water; vegetables contain eighty to ninety percent. Thus, we almost invariably take in too much liquid (yin).

[The original chart on page 50 said to "drink as little as possible." This advice, like Diet No. 7, has been taken to extremes and the current advice is, in most cases, to drink less but to drink when needed. -ed.]

To accelerate the macrobiotic cure, you had better drink less . . . enough less so that during a twenty-four hour period you urinate only twice if you are female or three times if you are male. [In other texts, Ohsawa says two to three times for females, three to four times for males, and more often for older folks. -ed.]

The drink-as-much-as-you-can system is a simpleminded invention because the originator of such a theory completely ignored the marvelous mechanism of kidney metabolism. He erred in conceiving the kidney to be similar in structure and function to a mechanical sewage system. Large quantities of liquid will flush out and clear a clay or cast iron pipe. The kidney, however, is not a cast iron pipe. It contains tissue that must be flexible and porous so that the processes of filtration, diffusion, and reabsorption can take place.

If liquid is taken in large quantities, the minute openings in the semi-permeable kidney tissue decrease in size (these openings are surrounded by tissue that is sponge-like, that soaks up liquid and swells) and little or no liquid can pass through. For all practical purposes, the kidneys are blocked. The net result is a complete reversal of what the drink-as-much-as-you-can system intended!

Help your tired, overworked kidneys: Drink less.

Delicious Macrobiotic Cuisine

Our macrobiotic cuisine, which can be so very delicious, requires a creative cook who also understands the art of yin-yang arrangement. Unfortunately, modern education neglects the creative capacity to such a degree that it is rare that we meet a good cook in the Occident.

Life is creative. To live is to create. Without creation we cannot exist, for our bodies create blood from our daily intake of food and beverages. Blood creates or motivates all our activities. Human adaptability is itself a result of this creative capacity. Life is the expression of creativity and in turn depends completely on the composition, proportion, preparation and the order of yin-yang elements in our eating and drinking.

Being a stranger to macrobiotic cooking, you will prepare foods that are not so delicious, at first. Never mind. Under these circumstances you will eat less — a vacation for your tired stomach and intestines. My congratulations!

Furthermore, your beginning meals will probably not be very well balanced. There is no need to worry, however. Through practice and the study of our theory, your judgment will develop rapidly: you will soon be a master of the art of balancing yin-yang elements in food preparation — the most basic art in your life.[19]

Good Things to Eat

Cereals (unrefined, whole grain): brown rice, buckwheat, wheat, corn, barley, millet, etc. Use them raw, cooked, creamed, with or without water, fried or baked. Eat as much as you like, provided that you chew thoroughly.

Vegetables: Any kind in season and local (excepting potato, tomato, and eggplant), such as carrots, onions, pumpkin, radish, cabbage, cauliflower, lettuce, etc., or wild vegetables such as dandelion, coltsfoot, burdock, shepherd's purse, watercress, etc.

CHAPTER 6

Macrobiotic Cuisine: Principal Food

The strangest thing in the Occident, it would appear to me, is the total absence of the most fundamental concept for living, namely principal food. My most significant discovery in America, fully as important as the one made by Christopher Columbus, is that here the idea of a principal food has entirely disappeared. No professor or man of medicine nowadays seems to be aware of its great value. By contrast, it has always been of primary consequence in the life of the Orient to the point that it was even deified in the beginnings of our history. The sages of the *Upanishads,* in their quest to know God, felt that grain represented the Creator. In accordance with this tradition, the orthodox Brahmin families of South India still offer a prayer to their rice before eating it.

The idea of principal food, the basis and significance of which is primarily biological and physiological, and only secondarily economical, geographical, and agricultural, is one of the most fundamental discoveries of man. It is fully as significant as the discovery of fire which enabled man to create civilization (the union of all religion, philosophy, science and technology) and which determined the history of the evolution of food in general.

Of course, one can live by eating almost anything that pleases either the sensory, sentimental, intellectual, economical, moral or ideological judgment. But there is a limit to such eating, namely unhappiness, which includes a variety of difficulties like slavery, illness, war and crime.

At one time, the clearly distinguished concept of principal and secondary food enabled the people of the Orient to live a relatively happy, free and peaceful life. That is, until the importation of the dazzling, violent Occidental civilization with its industrial and scientific devices. My personal experience proves this. In my childhood, however, that civilization penetrated our family life and destroyed it. I saw the death of my thirty-year-old mother, my two sisters, and my younger brother occur as a direct consequence of the introduction of Western foods and medicine into their lives. Then came my turn. Being a very poor orphan of ten, I fortunately could not continue the new Occidentalized food and medicine for financial reasons. Even so, I was dying at sixteen from the large quantities of chemically-refined sugar and sweets that I continued to use.

At eighteen, I discovered Oriental medicine, which is founded on the solid basis of Oriental cosmological philosophy some thousands of years old, and which cured me completely. For forty-eight years since, I have not been sick except for one occasion when I deliberately contracted the terrible (and usually incurable) disease named "tropical ulcers." This was at Dr. Schweitzer's hospital in Lambarene, Africa and was part of my quest for the biggest medical difficulties in the world. Through macrobiotic medicine I overcame this disease in a few days.

For forty-eight years I have unceasingly taught my physiological philosophy (the hygiene of Hygeia) to everyone that I have met. I have yet to meet a man who did not improve by following it absolutely and strictly. The only ones who cannot be cured are those who are unable to understand this pragmatic, simple and dialectical philosophy, the order of the universe and its unique principle.

Remember, at least sixty percent of your diet should consist of principal food. This is Diet No. 3 of the ten ways to health.

Macrobiotic Recipes

[The recipes that follow are from the original mimeograph edition of *Zen Macrobiotics*. Those new to macrobiotic cooking should see the discussion in the Preface to the Fourth Edition on pages 4 and 5 of this book. -ed.] By using these recipes and those in *The First Macrobiotic Cookbook* as a guide to the preparation of your daily meals, you can enjoy an endless variety of delicious dishes and at the same time achieve health and happiness.

Rice

1. Unpolished [Whole] Brown Rice

Rinse rice well in cold water. Add water in the amount of two to three times the amount of rice along with a small dash of salt. After the boiling point is reached, leave it over low heat for over one hour, ideally until the bottom of the rice is slightly scorched. The yellow part is the most yang and best because it is richest in minerals. It is the heaviest and the most nutritious. For this reason, it is especially good for sick and yinnized persons. (When a pressure cooker is used, the same amount of water as rice, or one-and-a-half times as much, is used.) After boiling, use very low heat for 20 or 25 minutes. Turn off heat and let stand for 10 to 20 minutes.

2. Sakura Rice

Add 5 to 10 percent pure traditionally prepared soy sauce to the rice in water and cook as in number 1.

3. Azuki Rice

Prepare rice as in number 1. Add azuki beans which have been partly cooked. Salt to taste and boil. (When a pressure cooker is used, you may add raw azuki beans to the rice in the beginning.)

4. Gomoku Rice

Mix 5 to 10 percent nitsuke vegetables with boiled rice.

5. Shahan Rice I

Add nitsuke vegetables to boiled rice as in number 4 and sauté in a very small amount of vegetable oil.

6. Shahan Rice II

Place nitsuke vegetables in a pan, add boiled rice, and sauté. Add a dash of salt.

7. Rice Croquettes

Mix nitsuke vegetables with boiled rice, add a little flour and a little water, make into balls, flatten, and fry in deep oil.

8. Rice Balls

Wet left hand with strong saline solution (5 percent salt), take about 2 heaping tablespoons of boiled rice, press right hand over it and shape into triangular balls. Sprinkle with a small amount of roasted sesame seeds.

9. Fried Rice Balls

Prepare rice balls as in number 8. Fry each rice ball in deep oil until both sides are crisply done.

10. Gomoku Rice Balls

Mix 5 to 10 percent nitsuke vegetables with boiled rice and shape into triangular rice balls as in number 8.

11. Sesame Rice

Add 10 percent roasted sesame seeds and a small amount of salt to rice and cook as in number 1.

12. Sesame Rice Balls

Mix 20 percent roasted sesame seeds and a little salt with boiled rice and shape into triangular balls.

13. Azuki Rice Balls

Prepare azuki rice as in number 3 and shape into balls.

14. Nori Seaweed Rice Balls

Wrap rice balls with toasted nori. These are very convenient for picnics and trips.

15. Tororo Seaweed Rice Balls

Coat rice balls with powered tororo or oboro seaweed.

16a. Umeboshi Rice Balls

Place one-fourth ounce umeboshi in the center of each rice ball. Not only is the flavor good, but the rice balls will not spoil for a few days, even in summer, and are good for trips.

16b. Whole Rice Kayu

Boil rice in 5 to 7 parts water with salt added. Good for sick people who have no appetite.

17. Nori Seaweed Rolled Rice

Toast nori lightly, place on bamboo mat, and spread boiled rice on nori evenly one-half inch thick. Place nitsuke carrots, burdock, lotus root, etc. in the center, roll from edge, cut into one-inch pieces, and place attractively on plate.

18. Gomoku Canapes

Arrange the following ingredients attractively in a rectangular box: 2 Julienne-cut carrots nitsuke, 2 thinly sliced lotus roots nitsuke, 2 beaten eggs fried in a thin layer, and shredded watercress nitsuke. On top of this press down boiled rice to a 2-inch thickness, invert over plate, cut into serving portions.

19. Chestnut Rice

Boil chestnuts until tender and then boil together with rice. When using a pressure cooker, mix uncooked chestnuts with rice and cook. Use about 10 to 20 percent chestnuts.

20. Miso Zosui

Make kayu (number 16b) and add miso in the proportion of 1 teaspoon miso to 1 tablespoon of raw rice. You can make this with cooked rice adding water and miso or miso soup. If you add one piece of roasted or fried mochi, it is delicious.

21. Cous-Cous Rice

Boil rice as usual. Sprinkle with cooked chickpeas and onions.

22a. Rice Cream

Toast rice until brown, grind into flour, and add 3 cups water to 4 tablespoons of rice. Boil about 25 minutes, adding water if necessary. Add salt to taste.

22b. Omedeto

Roast 5 ounces rice and add one-and-one-half ounces azuki beans. Cook with 12 parts water for about one hour or more. If a pressure cooker is used, use 5 to 6 parts of water. Add salt to taste. Very good for dessert.

23. Rice Potage

Thin rice cream (number 22a) with water and serve with bread croutons and minced parsley.

24. Fried Rice Flour Balls

Add a pinch of salt to rice flour, add enough water to form firm balls, and fry in oil.

Buckwheat

25. Kasha (Buckwheat)

Sauté 1 cup buckwheat in 1 tablespoon oil, add 2 cups water, and 1 level teaspoon salt. Boil slowly over low heat from the beginning. Serve with nitsuke vegetables, miso cream, miso, etc.

26. Buckwheat Croquettes

To boiled kasha add minced carrots, onions, etc., flour, a little water, and salt. Mix, form into balls, and fry in oil.

27. Fried Kasha

Mix boiled kasha, a little flour, minced onions, salt, and water. Fry, dropping it by spoon.

28. Kasha Gratin

Place boiled kasha in casserole. Bake until top has turned brown.

29. Buckwheat Kaki

Add two-and-a-half parts water to buckwheat flour, place over heat, stirring constantly until done. Serve with soy sauce.

30. Buckwheat Cream

Fry 2 heaping tablespoons of buckwheat flour in 1 tablespoon oil until well browned. Add 1 to 2 cups water, boil until thick, and add salt to taste. Pour into soup bowl and serve with croutons.

31. Fried Buckwheat I

Add one-and-one-half parts water to buckwheat flour, mix in a little salt, and fry in deep oil.

32. Fried Buckwheat II

Add minced onion to Fried Buckwheat I and fry.

33. Buckwheat Gratin

Sauté onions, carrots, and cauliflower in oil. Then, boil vegetables in a little water and add salt to taste. Place in casserole, pour over thin buckwheat cream (number 30), and bake in oven.

Noodles

34. Teuchi Buckwheat Noodles

To 1 pound buckwheat flour, add 1 egg (optional), 1 teaspoon salt, and a small amount of water. Knead until hard, then continue kneading until smooth and shiny. Roll out to about one-tenth inch in thickness, roll up, and slice as thin as possible. Drop into boiling water and boil until done. Drain and separate by pouring cold water over it and drain in a basket or colander. When dried buckwheat noodles are used, cook in boiling water. (The cooking water is served as a drink or used to cook vegetables as it contains very pure protein.)

35. Buckwheat Sauce

Mince 1 scallion, sauté in 1 teaspoon oil, add 3 cups water, add 3 inches of flat dried kombu, and boil well. Remove kombu, add 1 teaspoon salt and 5 tablespoons soy sauce, and remove from heat as soon as it returns to boil. Sauce should be somewhat salty, so salt to salty taste.

36. Kake Buckwheat Noodles

Place teuchi buckwheat noodles (number 34) in colander or basket, pour boiling water over it. Arrange in bowls and pour buckwheat sauce (number 35) over it.

37. Tempura Buckwheat Noodles

Heat teuchi buckwheat noodles (number 34) and put into bowls. Put shrimp or vegetable tempura on top and pour on buckwheat sauce (number 35).

38. Kitune Buckwheat Noodles

Heat teuchi buckwheat noodles (number 34) and put into bowls. Place thin fried bean curds, boiled scallions, etc. on top and pour on buckwheat sauce (number 35).

39. Ankake Buckwheat Noodles

Heat teuchi buckwheat noodles (number 34), and put into bowls. Sauté scallions, carrots, cabbage, etc. in oil. Add buckwheat sauce (number 35). Add a little kuzu flour paste made by mixing the flour with water little by little. Boil until thickened. Pour the mixture over the buckwheat noodles.

40. Yaki Buckwheat Noodles

Fry teuchi buckwheat noodles (number 34) in a small amount oil, place on dish, and pour vegetable ankake (see number 39) on top.

41. Miso on Sarashina

Prepare sauce of miso and sesame butter. Place buckwheat noodles on plate and pour sauce over it.

42. Buckwheat Noodles Gratin

Sauté onion, carrots, cauliflower, etc. in oil. Prepare bechamel sauce (number 219), blend with vegetables, and add salt to taste. Place buckwheat noodles in casserole, pour the vegetable mixture over noodles, and bake in oven.

43. Macaroni, Udon, Vermicelli, Etc.

Boil desired noodles, drain, and wash in cold water. These noodles may be prepared the same ways as buckwheat noodles.

Millet and Others

44. Millet

Sauté 1 cup millet in 2 tablespoons oil and add a little salt and 4 parts of water. Place over medium heat, lower heat when it boils. Simmer a long time until soft. Serve with miso cream, nitsuke vegetables, or miso. This millet can be substituted for kasha in kasha croquettes, fried kasha, etc.

45. Cous-Cous

Cous-cous may be steamed or boiled like kasha. Boil minced onions until well done, add a small quantity of oil, and add salt when tender. Serve together. (This is Arabian cooking.) Cous-cous may be bought in a store. Otherwise coarse wheat flour may be used.

46. Bulgur

Prepare cous-cous in the same way as Kasha (number 25). (This is Armenian cooking.) Coarse wheat meal which has been steamed and dried can be purchased in stores.

47. Oatmeal

Prepare in the same way as number 44. Do not use milk.

Raw Rice, Etc.

48a. Raw Rice

Take one handful of raw rice instead of breakfast for a few days. By this method, you can expel all the parasites in your intestines, particularly the duodenum. You will be astonished to see so many of them emerge. I know of no treatment that is more effective. Be sure to chew each mouthful of rice at least one hundred times.

48b. Grilled Rice

Roast rice in frying pan until well browned. Eat without cooking. This preparation is good as the treatment for hyper-insulinism and rheumatism.

49. Hokkaido Pumpkin Seeds

Spray seeds with salted water and heat well. Or fry them in a little oil, adding a pinch of salt. They can be used as a dessert, in the manner of the Chinese. This is an effective way to expel parasites, especially the tapeworm.

50. Gomashio (salt and sesame seeds)

Heat 5 tablespoons of sesame seeds. Crush them gently in a mortar with a pestle (or suribachi). Add 1 tablespoon of sea salt, heat again, and recrush until a well-mixed but coarse powder results. Eat this with rice and/or bread every day. Use as a condiment and sprinkle over all foods to taste.

Keep mixture in a tightly closed bottle. See *The First Macrobiotic Cookbook* for more detailed instructions.

51. Umeboshi

These Japanese salted plums are preserved for at least three years and are very yangizing. In Japan, all traditional families prepare this every year. Available at natural food stores.

CHAPTER 7

Macrobiotic Cuisine: Secondary Foods

[Most of the recipes in this chapter were omitted from the Oles' 1965 edition. They have been added here because of the great interest in knowing the recipes that Ohsawa originally included in the original manuscript of *Zen Macrobiotics*. All the recipes can be prepared tastefully once the basics of macrobiotic cooking are mastered. Also, you will want to vary the amounts of salt and oil depending on your own needs. Quantity always affects quality. If you eat very few vegetables, as Ohsawa apparently did in his daily eating, the individual vegetable dishes can be more salty and oily as they are written here. However, the current recommendations are to eat more vegetables prepared with less salt and oil. -ed.]

Nitsukes and Nishime

61. Carrot and Sesame Nitsuke

Cut 2 carrots as small as possible. Sauté well in 1 tablespoon oil. Add roasted sesame seeds, mix, and add salt to taste. All nitsukes are prepared slightly salty.

62. Endive Nitsuke

Cut 5 endive in half lengthwise, sauté in 2 tablespoons oil, add 1 level teaspoon salt, cover, and boil over low heat until tender. Add a dash of soy sauce.

63. Kinpira
Sliver burdock roots and carrots separately in the proportion of 3 to 1. Sauté burdock in oil until well done, add carrots, and cook until tender in a little water. Season with salt and soy sauce.

64. Onion Nitsuke
Slice 2 large onions lengthwise and sauté well in 1 tablespoon oil. Season with salt, adding a small amount of soy sauce last.

65. Watercress Nitsuke
Cut watercress into 1-inch pieces and sauté in oil using low heat. Add salt to taste. If a little tahini is added the flavor is enhanced.

66. Cabbage with Onion Nitsuke
Prepare in the same manner as numbers 64 and 65.

67. Carrots with Onion Nitsuke
Prepare in the same manner as numbers 61 and 64.

68. Celery with Scallions Nitsuke
Sauté celery and scallions in oil and add salt to taste. The various kinds of nitsuke mentioned above should not be juicy. Foods that are juicy cannot be called nitsuke.

69. Nishime
Cut carrots or burdock roots, lotus root, white radish, fried

bean curds, Simikon, and Yuba into large pieces, add water, and boil until very tender. Season with salt and soy sauce. This, too, should not be juicy when done.

Soup and Other Dishes

70. Russian Soup

Cut 3 onions in quarters and sauté in oil. Add a little cabbage that has been cut into one-half inch squares and continue to sauté. Add 1 thinly sliced carrot and enough water to cover. Roast until carrots are crisp, add salt to taste, and boil over medium heat for a long time. Add a little water. When the soup thickens, season well with salt.

71. "Jardinier"

Cut whites of scallions, carrots, cauliflower, etc. and sauté in oil. Add water and boil until tender. Season with salt. (The greens of the scallions may be used for nitsuke.)

72. Au Polenta

Cut white turnips, carrots, onions, cabbage, etc. in large pieces and sauté in oil. Add water to cover vegetables fully; boil until tender. Brown 3 heaping tablespoons of polenta in 3 tablespoons oil, mix into thin paste with water, pour into vegetable mixture, and boil slowly over low heat. Season with salt. (Polenta is coarsely ground corn and can be purchased in natural food stores.)

73. Soup de Millet

Prepare in the same manner as Au Polenta (number 72) using millet flour in place of polenta.

74. Vegetable Stew

Sauté turnips, onions, carrots, cauliflower, etc. in oil; then boil. When tender pour in flour that has been roasted in oil and mixed with water.

75. Vegetable Gratin

Boil vegetables as for soup and place in casserole dish. Over this pour polenta, millet flour, or buckwheat flour, etc. that has been prepared in the same manner as bechamel sauce (number 219). Bake in oven.

76. Pumpkin Potage

Cut an onion into small pieces and sauté in oil. Cut 1 pound of pumpkin or squash and add. Boil in about half the amount of water until tender. Strain and season with salt to taste. Brown 4 tablespoons flour in oil, mix with water, blend into pumpkin mixture, and boil. Serve with croutons, parsley etc. If you make this with Hokkaido pumpkin you will be surprised, it is so delicious.

77. Carrot Potage

Prepare in the same manner as number 76 substituting carrots for the pumpkin or squash.

78. Tempura

Slice carrots, scallions, etc. into thin slices, dip in flour-and-water batter (one-and-one-half times as much water as flour), add a dash of salt and dry in deep oil by spoonfuls.

79. Tempura Vegetables

Watercress, cauliflower, endive, burdock root, lotus root, celery, pumpkin, etc. are used for tempura in the same way as carrots in number 78.

80. Lotus Root Balls

Grate lotus root, add half as much minced onion, and mix. Season with salt. Add flour to hold together and fry in deep oil. (This recipe is especially helpful in cases of asthma, diabetes, polio, arthritis, etc.)

81. Lotus Root Balls a la Bechamel Sauce

Place lotus root balls (number 80) gently in bechamel sauce (number 219) on plate and sprinkle with minced celery. When tempura vegetables (number 79) are served in this manner the flavor is greatly enhanced. Millet, buckwheat, or other flour can be used for bechamel sauce.

82. Baked Pumpkin

Cut pumpkin into large pieces, sprinkle with a little salt, and bake in oven. Serve with miso sauce or soy sauce.

83. Boiled Pumpkin with Miso

Cut pumpkin into large pieces. Mince onions and sauté in oil. Add pumpkin. Add water and a dash of salt. Boil until tender. Add miso diluted with water to the vegetables.

84. Boiled Pumpkin

Cut Japanese kuri squash or Hokkaido pumpkin into large pieces. Mince onions, prepare as in number 83. Season only with a little salt and boil until tender.

85. Lotus Root Ankake

Cut lotus root, carrot, white radish (daikon), etc. in rectangular pieces and sauté in oil. Add a little water and cook until tender. Dilute kuzu flour with water and mix into vegetable mixture to thicken.

86. Turnip Ankake

Sauté whole round turnips in oil. Then boil in enough water until tender. Season with salt and thicken with kuzu flour and water mixture. Add a little soy sauce last.

87. Kuzu Gruel

Mix kuzu flour with water: 1 heaping tablespoon kuzu to 5 ounces water. Place over flame and stir constantly until thickened and clear. Season with natural soy sauce and a pinch of salt.

When appetite is poor because of a cold, kuzu gruel will improve the condition surprisingly. Genuine kuzu flour is available at natural food stores.

88. Cracknel Yuba

Bean curds, tofu, etc. These items may also be prepared as Ankake (see number 85).

Pie

89. Pumpkin Pie

Start with 1 pound of sliced pumpkin and diced onions. Sauté onions in 1 tablespoon oil, add sliced pumpkin, and boil in a little water. Add salt and sieve to a cream consistency. To prepare pie crust, mix 1 cup flour, 3 tablespoons oil, one-half teaspoon salt, 1 teaspoon cinnamon, and 1 teaspoon minced orange rind and blend in a small amount of water to form a soft dough. (If using whole grain flour, sieve to remove any hulls or husk; use the residue for tempura, bread, croquettes, etc.—do not discard. For oil, use equal parts of corn and sesame oil, olive and sesame oil, or sunflower and sesame oil.) Roll out to one-fifth inch thickness and line pie plate. Fill crust with pumpkin mixture about 1-inch deep and top with 1 diced apple (omit apple for sick people). Cover with crust, press down edges, using a fork slash top with an attractive design, and brush with one egg yolk. Cut cross in center with a knife. Bake in oven until lightly browned and crisp.

90. Chestnut Apple Pie
Boil chestnuts until tender. Mix cinnamon, orange rind, salt, and make pie crust as in number 89. Prepare pie filling in the same way as in number 89.

91. Ogura Pie
For cream filling, boil azuki beans, season lightly with salt, fill crust, and bake. This recipe is permissible for sick people (with or without chestnuts).

92. Rice Pie
This may be used as a staple food and is permissible for sick people. Mix boiled rice with vegetable nitsuke (carrots, lotus roots, onions, watercress, etc.). Add a little flour. Prepare pie as in number 89 and bake.

93. Sweet Potato Chestnut Pie
Boil sweet potatoes and sieve. Add a little salt. Boil chestnuts and add to sweet potatoes. Fill crust and bake. This recipe is not for sick people.

94. Vegetable Pie
Sauté carrots, onion, cabbage, cauliflower, etc. in oil, then

boil in water until tender. Line pie plate with crust and fill with the vegetables. Into nitsuke juice, blend flour that has been browned in a little oil, and thicken. Pour this sauce over filling instead of covering with crust and bake.

95. Onion and Carrot Pie

Prepare crust and line pie plate. Using one-third the amount of carrots as onions, sauté both in oil and then season with salt. Add one beaten egg, fill the pie shell, and bake.

96. Apple Pie

Line pie plate with crust. Cut 3 apples in crescent shapes. Place in shell attractively like a round flower. Sprinkle with salt and bake until top is browned. Mix kuzu flour in water and place over heat until thickened. Pour over apples attractively and cool. Agar-agar or gelatin may be used instead of kuzu although kuzu is preferred.

97. Plum Pie

Remove pits from dried plums and boil plums until tender in a little water. Add a dash of salt and cinnamon. Prepare pie as in number 89 and bake.

98. Apple and Chestnut Kinton

Use chestnuts and apples in the proportion of 3 to 1. Boil chestnuts and put one-third aside. Add apples that have been sliced and boil until done. Sieve, then add remaining whole chestnuts. This recipe is not for sick people.

Gyoza and Chapati

99. Piroshki Fried Pie

Prepare pie crust and cut into round pieces, 3 to 4 inches in diameter. Sliver carrots, onions, watercress, etc. in thin pieces and sauté in oil. Add boiled rice, season with salt, and sauté well. Form small balls with hands and place on pieces of crust. Fold over crust and press down edge with a fork. Fry in oil. Prepare different piroshki using various ingredients as above by baking instead of frying. Brush with egg yolk for an attractive result. Small individual pie plates may be used for a different effect. Children enjoy individual pies. This recipe is permissible for sick people.

100. Gyoza

Add a little salt to flour and knead with water to form a soft dough. Roll out very thin and cut into round pieces 2 to 3 inches in diameter. Dice vegetables, sauté, season with salt, add a little flour, and mix. Wrap vegetable mixture in pieces of dough in long narrow shapes. Cook until done in boiling water. Serve with soy sauce, miso cream (number 202), etc.

101. Fried Gyoza

Fry already boiled gyoza in a little oil until crisp.

102. Deep Fried Gyoza

Fry already boiled gyoza in deep oil.

103. Gyoza Gratin

Place fried gyoza in baking dish. Prepare rice cream, millet cream, etc. rather thin and pour over gyoza and bake in oven. When there are visitors, you may add a little shrimp, white-meat fish or fowl. For sick people, dough is made from buckwheat flour.

104. Chapati

Add a small amount of salt to flour, knead with water to form a soft dough. Make round balls 1 tablespoonful at a time. Roll into round pieces and bake in oven. Or, instead of baking they can be puffed by holding them over a flame. Serve with nitsuke vegetables. This recipe is good for those who are sick or yin as a staple food. Those made with buckwheat, rye, or millet flour are very yang and good for those who are ill.

105. Puri

Chapati should be rolled into small round pieces. Fry in deep oil and they will puff up like balloons. Serve with nitsuke vegetables. In India, chapati made with whole wheat flour is eaten every day.

Jinenjo (Wild Potato)

106. Jinenjo

Cube jinenjo into 1-inch pieces and sprinkle with salt. Fry in deep oil. Then cook with soy sauce in a pan.

107. Jinenjo Hamburg

Grate jinenjo, chop onions or scallions, and mix. Season with salt. Using quite a large amount of oil in a frying pan, cover and fry until soft and fluffy.

108. Jinenjo Balls

Prepare as in number 107 and drop by spoon into deep oil and fry.

109. Jinenjo Gratin

Place ingredients as in number 107 in a casserole dish.
Bake in oven.

110. Tororo (Grated Jinenjo)

Grate jinenjo and place in a small dish. Sprinkle toasted
nori on top and serve with soy sauce.

111. Tororo Soup

Grate jinenjo and mix with soup stock or miso soup.

Beans

112. Pois Chickpeas

Wash chickpeas and soak in hot water overnight. Boil until
tender. Season with salt. Serve with juice or serve after boiling
so that no liquid remains.

113. Beignet Chickpeas

Add flour to boiled chickpeas to thicken. Add water when
there is no liquid. Season with salt. Drop with tablespoon to
fry in oil.

114. Chana Balls

Mix chana flour (Indian grain) with water to make batter.
Season with salt. Mince onion and add to batter. Fry in deep
oil dropping by spoon. Mashed boiled chickpeas can be used
instead of chana flour.

115. Pakodi

Mix water with chana flour to form batter. Season with
salt. (Grated or cut onions are generally added to this.) Fry in

deep oil dropping it by spoon.

116. Chickpea Croquettes
Mix flour with boiled chickpeas. Form into balls and flatten. Coat with bread crumbs and fry in deep oil.

117. Boiled Soybeans with Miso
Roast soybeans in pan until they pop. Thin miso with water and add to beans. Add a small amount of water, cover the pan, and let steam until tender. Remove cover and boil until the liquid is gone.

118. Boiled Beans
Boil soybeans until tender. Season with soy sauce and salt. Boil until liquid is gone. Prepare black beans in the same way.

119. Gomoku Beans
Boil soybeans until tender. Dice white radish (daikon), carrots, burdock root, lotus root, etc. and sauté in oil. Add to beans and boil until tender. Season with salt and soy sauce.

120. Goziru Soup
Soak soybeans overnight. Mash soybeans until creamy. Prepare soup with onions, carrots, white radish (daikon), etc. Pour grated beans into soup and boil well. Season with salt and soy sauce.

121. Azuki Beans
Boil azuki beans until tender. Season with salt, boil until thick. When pounded rice cake (mochi) is available, broil and add.

122. Mashed Azuki Beans

Boil azuki beans until tender. Season with salt. Remove liquid and mash.

123. Mottled Kidney Beans

Boil the beans (or peas) in water and season with salt. Add a little oil.

124. String Beans

Sauté whole string beans in oil. Add water and simmer slowly. Season with salt and soy sauce, rather strongly. Cook until liquid is gone and string beans are wrinkled.

Corn

125. Corn

Scrape kernels off 3 ears of corn with a knife or grate with a coarse grater. Mince 1 onion, sauté in 1 tablespoon oil, and add corn and 3 parts water. Add salt and simmer over low heat until soft. Stir gently occasionally to prevent scorching. Add 1 heaping tablespoon kuzu mixed with a little water. Add a little soy sauce last. Float nori, croutons, etc. on top and serve.

126. Roasted Corn

Roast young ears of corn over fire or in the oven. Coat with soy sauce, roast for a short time, and serve.

127. Boiled Corn

Boil corn in a 4 percent salt solution. Serve with soy sauce.

128. Beignet Corn

Cut kernels off of young corn, mash a little, immerse in

tempura batter, and fry in deep oil. Serve with soy sauce.

129. Corn Dumpling

Knead corn flour with water and make small round dumplings. Boil and skewer. Broil a short time. Serve with miso, azuki beans, etc.

130. Cream of Corn

Add a little salt to corn flour and knead with hot water. Mix into soup stock or miso soup. Stir gently until done.

131. Corn Croquettes

Mix a little salt, cinnamon, and water in corn flour and knead. Shape into croquettes and fry in a small amount of oil.

132. Crepes de Mais

Brown cornmeal in a small amount of oil. Add water and make thin batter. Put a little oil in frying pan and pour in a thin layer of the mixture. Fry until crisp on both sides. Serve with nitsuke vegetables.

Miscellaneous and Salads

133. Ogura Vermicelli

Boil azuki beans until tender and creamy. Season with salt. Mix with boiled vermicelli and heat thoroughly in a pan. Pour into rectangular mold and chill until firm. Remove from mold and cut into rectangular pieces for hot weather. Can be served hot in cold weather.

134. Lotus Root with Azuki

Prepare lotus root in the nitsuke style (see number 61).

Add boiled azuki beans and season with salt.

135. Sesame Curds (Goma Tofu)

Roast sesame seeds until well done and grind. Mix 3 heaping tablespoons of kuzu flour with water and boil for a long time until it spins into a thread. Add sesame and season with salt. Pour into rectangular pan and let sit until firm. This can be made easily with tahini. Serve with soy sauce, miso, etc.

136. Aemono (Salad)

Roast sesame seeds well. Grind until creamy. Add soy sauce and a little water to make thick cream. Boil scallions, onions, white radish (daikon), carrots, cabbage, watercress, spinach, cauliflower, or pumpkin, etc. in salted water. Mix with sesame cream. Miso may be substituted for sesame seeds. Do not discard vegetable liquid, rather utilize it in soups.

137. Vegetable and Fruit Salad

Shred cabbage and carrots. Cut up cauliflower and apple into small pieces and put aside. Mix well 4 tablespoons oil, 1 tablespoon salt, and 1 egg. Pour boiling water over cabbage and carrots. Boil cauliflower in salted water. Soak apples in salted water. Mix these vegetables with oil mixture, and mound attractively on large platter lined with lettuce. This is served after meat dishes.

138. Chou Farcie

This is a country dish from the French buckwheat producing region. Separate cabbage leaves one at a time carefully and wash. Mix buckwheat in twice the amount of water. Season with salt. Beat 2 eggs. In a covered iron pan, using plenty of oil, lay a leaf of cabbage on the bottom, pour in a layer of buckwheat mixture, add a layer of egg, then a layer of cabbage. Alternate in this manner, with a cabbage leaf on top. Cover and bake in a moderate oven for one-and-a-half hours. Remove from pan by inverting over platter. Cut at the table while hot. Serve with miso sauce, soy sauce, etc.

139. Buckwheat Crepes

Mix buckwheat flour in 3 parts of water. Add 1 egg and stir well. Put oil in a frying pan, pour in a thin layer of mixture, fry on both sides, and fold in quarters. Mound attractively on plate. Before folding, fill crepes with nitsuke vegetables and miso. They may be served without the nitsuke filling as a staple food. For an inbetween meal snack, they may be filled with chestnuts, plums, raisins, or jam.

Wild and Marine Vegetables

There are thousands of edible wild plants, leaves, roots, buds, flowers, grains, seeds, etc., all produced by God without any commercial intention. They are pure and free from chemical fertilizers or insecticides, for in nature there are no poisons at all, only too much yang or yin, both of which can be neutralized by macrobiotic cooking. These natural foods can be used to cure yin or yang diseases. Here are just a few: aoza (wild spinach), akaza (pigweed), dandelion, nazuna (shepherd's purse), nobiru (wild scallions), huki (coltsfoot), and gobo (burdock). All of them are very delicious and medicinally very useful.

Also, there are so many marine plants (seaweeds). Kombu, nori, wakame, hijiki, arame, etc. Tororo as it is used here refers to the inner part of kombu that has been finely grated. (Tororo also refers to a wild potato.) Oboro refers to the whole kombu plant that has been grated.

150. Shio Kombu

Take a thick piece of kombu and wash it in water. Keep this water for cooking later as it contains many minerals. Cut the kombu into 1-inch squares. Add 3 parts of water and cook well until it becomes soft. Add salt and cook until it becomes dry. Add 10 to 20 percent of natural soy sauce and cook until it becomes dry. This preparation is very good for arthritis, high or low blood pressure, other cardiac problems, goiter, tumors, etc.

151. Kombu-Maki

Take a rather thin piece of kombu and cut it into 4-inch squares. Cut carrots, burdock, lotus root to the same length as the kombu and roll them with kombu 2 times and tie up all with kampyo (a cord made of a kind of pumpkin). Cook them well with the water in which you washed the kombu. It takes a long time. Add salt and soy sauce to taste.

152. Fried Kombu

Cut thick pieces of kombu in 3-inch squares, fry in oil, and add salt. This is good for dessert.

153. Musubi Kombu

Cut kombu the size of your small finger. Tie each strip in a knot and fry.

154. Kombu Soup

Make a soup of kombu (4 by 10 inches) with a quart of water. This makes enough soup for five persons. Add a little salt. You can put in any vegetables you like and add a little soy sauce.

155. Matuba Kombu

Cut kombu in three inch by one-fifth inch pieces and split each like pine needles and fry.

156. Salmon Head Kombu Maki

Cut salted dry salmon head and wrap in a piece of kombu as in number 151. Cook this well without adding any salt. Add a little natural soy sauce. This preparation is good for polio, paralysis, and decalcifying diseases.

157. Hijiki with Lotus Root

Soak 1 ounce hijiki in water for 5 minutes. Cut in small pieces. Cut 2 ounces lotus root and fry in 2 tablespoons of oil. Add the hijiki and its soaking water. Add 1 teaspoon salt and cook for a long time until the water has evaporated. Add soy sauce and cook a little longer.

158. Hijiki Nitsuke

Soak hijiki in water. Cut it into small pieces. Fry well in 2 tablespoons of oil and add a little water. Then add soy sauce.

159. Hijiki with Agé

Prepare hijiki as in number 158. Add agé (a fried soybean product), cutting it into small pieces. Cook with a little water and soy sauce.

160. Hijiki and Soybeans

Prepare just like number 157, add well-cooked soybeans, and add soy sauce.

161. Gomoku Hijiki

Dice carrots, lotus root, and burdock root and cut hijiki as in number 157. Fry mixture in 3 tablespoons of oil.

162. Hijiki rice

Mix hijiki as prepared in number 158 to cooked rice.

163. Dandelion Leaves Nitsuke

Wash dandelion leaves well and cut into small pieces. Prepare in nitsuke style (see number 62) and add salt or soy sauce.

164. Dandelion Root

Wash roots well; do not peel. Cut into thin round pieces. Cook well 1 cup of roots in 1 tablespoon of oil. Add salt and soy sauce. This recipe is good for arthritis, cardiac problems, polio, rheumatism, etc.

165. Aoza (Wild Spinach)

Prepare in nitsuke style (see number 62) and add soy sauce.

166. Huki (Coltsfoot)

Take stems of huki and cook with a little water and soy sauce for a long time. (You may prepare the leaves also by cutting them into small pieces and preparing as a nitsuke.) This you can preserve a long time as with all nitsuke vegetables.

Miso

201. Miso Sauce

Mix 1 big tablespoon of miso and 3 tablespoons of sesame butter. Add 1 cup of water, mix, and cook. When cooked, add 1 teaspoon of minced orange peel and mix. Use this sauce with rice, buckwheat grain or noodles, vermicelli, vegetables, etc.

202. Miso Cream

Use a little less water than in number 201. Use this cream as in number 201. It can be a substitute for butter and cheese.

203. Muso

Mix 1 tablespoon miso with 4 tablespoons of sesame butter or tahini. Add a little minced orange peel. Use as a spread on rice, bread, etc.

204. Miso Soup (5 persons)

Heat 1 tablespoon sesame or olive oil. Add 1 cup minced onion and 1 minced cabbage leaf. When these are well cooked, add one-third cup carrots (cut in small pieces), and cook well. Add 4 cups of water. Last of all add a little diluted miso. Then add a little minced raw onion and roasted nori.

205. Carrots and Onion au Miso (15 persons)

Mince 2 or 3 onions and cook in 1 tablespoon of oil. Cut 1 carrot in small pieces and add. Cook well in a little water and add miso. Use as a condiment.

206. Vegetables au Miso

Quarter 2 onions and cook in 2 tablespoons of oil. Add 4

sliced cabbage leaves and cook well. Add 1 sliced carrot and
then add 2 cups of water. Then add miso diluted in a little water and a little salt.

207. Oden au Miso

Place whole onions, and white radishes (daikon), albi, and
carrots cut in big pieces on a sheet of kombu in a pan and add
water. Cook well with a little salt. Place on bamboo skewers,
adding scallions and miso. The longer you cook these, the
more delicious they become.

208. Buckwheat Dango au Miso

Make balls of buckwheat and cook them in water. Put
them on bamboo skewers (5 to a skewer). Cover these balls
with a little miso cream (number 202) and heat over a flame.
(You can use other creams too.)

209. Miso-Ae

Cook carrots, onion, watercress, cauliflower, radishes, endive, celery, etc. in water and serve with miso cream.

210. Tekka No. 1

Mince 1 ounce of lotus root, one-and-a-half ounces of burdock root, 1 ounce of carrot, and one-fifth ounce of ginger.
First, fry burdock root in 2 ounces of oil. Then, add carrots
and lotus root and cook well. Then add ginger and miso. Add
2 more ounces of oil and cook until dry. This recipe is good
for all yin diseases.

211. Tekka No. 2

Mince 2 ounces of lotus root, one-half ounce burdock root,
one-half ounce carrot, and one-fifth ounce of dandelion root

and prepare as in number 210. This preparation is good for coughs, asthma, tuberculosis, etc.

Soy Sauce

Use traditional (natural) soy sauce in all cooking (vegetables and fish). Soy sauce diluted with a little water is very good with sashimi and fried oysters, tempura, sukiyaki, tofu, etc.

212. Sakura Rice
Boil rice with 5 percent soy sauce. This is very appetizing.

213. Sauce au Soy Sauce
Mince one onion and fry in 1 tablespoon of oil. Add 1 cup of water and 3 tablespoons of sesame butter or tahini and mix well. Add one-half teaspoon of salt and cook well.

214. Sauce au Sesame
Grill one-and-a-half ounces of sesame seeds, then crush until it becomes oily. Add 1 to 2 ounces of soy sauce. This preparation is good served on cooked vegetables, and also on rice, bread, sandwiches, etc.

215. Bouillon au Soy Sauce
Mince one-half onion and fry in 1 teaspoon of oil. Add 2 cups of water. When cooked, season it with soy sauce.

216. Ositasi
Boil watercress, spinach, lettuce, cabbage, or any other vegetables. Serve them with soy sauce.

217. Oatmeal Cream

Cook well 4 tablespoons of oatmeal with 1 tablespoon of oil. Add soy sauce and a little salt. Add water to taste.

218. Oatmeal Potage

Add water to number 217 to make a potage. Sprinkle with minced parsley, watercress, or some other green vegetable. You can make the same things (potage or cream) with rice, wheat, kokkoh, or buckwheat flour.

219. Bechamel Sauce a la Soy Sauce

Add water to 1 heaping tablespoon flour and 1 tablespoon oil and cook. Then add soy sauce.

220. Mayonnaise a la Soy Sauce

Mix 1 egg yolk with a little salt, adding oil little by little. Add hot water, then add minced parsley. Serve this with any boiled vegetable or fish.

221. Lyonnaise Sauce

Fry minced onion in a little oil. Add vin blanc (white wine). Add 2 to 3 tablespoons of bechamel sauce (number 219). Good with grilled fish.

Beverages

301. Rice Tea

Roast rice until brown. To 1 tablespoon of rice add 10 times as much water. Bring to a boil. Add pinch of salt and serve. This roasted rice may be used as a staple food. Roasted rice and roasted bancha tea may be mixed to make a delicious beverage.

302. Wheat Tea

Roast wheat until brown. Boil 1 heaping tablespoon in 5 ounces of water. In summer, serve cold.

303. Dandelion Coffee

Wash and dry dandelion roots. Cut into small pieces. Saute in frying pan with small amount of oil. Grind in coffee grinder. To 1 teaspoon add 1 cup of water. Boil for 10 minutes. Strain and serve. Chicory may be added for those who prefer a bitter flavor.

304. Ohsawa Coffee (Yannoh)

Take 3 tablespoons rice, 2 tablespoons wheat, 2 tablespoons azuki, 1 tablespoon chickpeas and 1 tablespoon chicory. Roast separately until well browned. Mix together and brown in 1 tablespoon oil. Cool and grind into powder. Prepare beverage to desired strength. Use 1 tablespoon to 15 ounces water. Boil 10 minutes, strain and serve.

305. Kokkoh

This is a mixture of roasted rice, glutinous (sweet) rice, oatmeal, soybeans and sesame seeds that have been ground together. It is easiest to use the factory-made product. Use 1 heaping tablespoon to 11 ounces of water. Stir and boil for 10 minutes.

306. Mugwort Tea

Pick 1 ounce of mugwort leaves and boil in 5 ounces water. Add salt. Use this as a drink before breakfast. Effectively eliminates round worms. Dried mugwort leaves will keep for years.

307. Mint Tea

Use mint leaves in the same way as number 306.

308. Tilleul Tea

Boil tilleul [Linden, I think. -ed.] leaves and serve as beverage.

309. Mu Tea

Boil 1 packet of mu tea in 32 ounces of water for 10 to 20 minutes and serve. This can be used every day for yin sick people by boiling down the above recipe to 16-20 ounces. Use this as the total liquid for 2 days. Can be reheated without impairing either the quality or flavor. Mu tea contains ginseng root plus 15 medicinal plants and is the most yang beverage.

310. Bancha Tea

Roast coarse bancha tea (the leaves and twigs must be 3 years old on the bush) until browned. Boil a heaping tablespoon in 24 ounces of water for 10 minutes.

311. Sho-Ban (Bancha Tea with Soy Sauce)

Fill tea cup about one tenth with soy sauce. Add hot tea as above (number 310) and serve. This beverage is effective for eliminating fatigue, after injuries, and for the relief of heart distress.

313. Yang-Yang Tea

This must be used only for those who are very, very yin. [There are no instructions given in the original manuscript.]

314. Dragon Tea

This tea is good for extremely yin persons, especially those vomiting, with morning sickness, or leukorrhea. [There are no instructions given in the original manuscript.]

315. Haru Tea
This tea has a very good flavor and is good for head colds. [There are no instructions given in the original manuscript.]

316. Kohren Tea
This is made from dried, ground lotus root and can be purchased from natural food stores or prepared at home. Steep 1 teaspoonful of the powder in 1 cup freshly boiling water. Take 3 times a day, eliminating all other liquids. Good for coughs, whooping cough, asthma, and tuberculosis.

317. Kuzu Drink
Dilute 1 heaping teaspoon of kuzu (chunks) in one-half tablespoon of water. Add one-and-one-quarter cups of water; boil gently, stirring constantly until transparent. Season with a little soy sauce to taste. This is a good drink for everyone and especially good in cases of diarrhea or head cold.

318. Renkon (Lotus) Tea
Crush a 2-inch piece of raw lotus root; squeeze out the juice. Add 10 percent grated raw ginger, a pinch of salt, and boil in the same manner as in number 317.

319. Azuki Juice
Boil 1 tablespoon azuki beans in 2 quarts of water. Boil down to 1 quart of liquid and add a pinch of salt. This juice is very good for kidney trouble.

320. Radish Drink No. 1

Grate 2 tablespoons of white radish (daikon). Add one-and-a-half pints of hot water, 2 tablespoons soy sauce and 1 teaspoon of grated, raw ginger. For a cold, take this in bed; you will perspire (or urinate) in lowering your fever.

321. Radish Drink No. 2

Grate white radish and squeeze out the juice. To one-fourth pint of juice add one-half pint of water and a little salt. Boil for a few minutes. Drink this once per day for only 3 days. Good for swollen legs.

322. Ransho (Soy Sauce and Egg)

Carefully crack open a fertilized egg so that the shell breaks into equal parts. Beat egg well. Fill one of the shell halves with soy sauce and add to egg. Beat again. Swallow this mixture without tasting. Take this once a day before going to bed and for only 3 days. Very good for severe heart trouble.

[This preparation is very strong and should be used only in cases of yin heart trouble. If you have any question, consult your health-care advisor or see *Natural Healing from Head to Toe* by Cornellia and Herman Aihara. -ed.]

323. Soba Tea

Save the water that buckwheat is cooked in. Add soy sauce and salt to taste.

324. Umeboshi Juice

Boil 3 or 4 umeboshi plums in 2 pints of water. Put through sieve. Add 2 pints of water. Take this cool for a delicious summer drink.

325. Ume-Sho-Kuzu Drink

Crush 1 umeboshi plum in one-half pint of water. Mix 1 heaping teaspoon kuzu in 1 tablespoonful of water and add to the umeboshi water. Add 1 teaspoon grated raw ginger and another pint of water. Boil mixture until it thickens. Add 3 teaspoons of soy sauce. This drink is good for colds.

326. Special Rice Cream Drink

Wash, dry in flat pan, and roast 1 cup of brown rice. Boil this in 2 quarts of water for 1 to 2 hours, the longer the better. Strain through a cheesecloth-lined sieve or make a triangle of cheesecloth large enough to hold in hand when filled with above mixture. Squeeze mixture through the cloth in the same manner that you would use a cake decorator. Save the rice pulp that remains after squeezing for use in baking bread, etc. The rice juice is good as a breakfast for sick people. It is also useful as afternoon tea for those who are tired.

CHAPTER 8

Macrobiotic Cuisine: Special Dishes

Animal Products

As a general rule, Buddhism forbids the use of all foods derived from animals. This is particularly true for Zen Buddhism which is a more advanced branch of religion, biologically speaking. Thus, without macrobiotics, there is no Buddhism!

Since macrobiotics is not the kind of vegetarianism that is mere sentimentality, hemoglobinic foods are avoided for biological and physiological reasons, only. They are avoided in order to develop men who can think.

Animal meat has the ideal composition for an animal; animal glands produce hormones fit for creatures who act only according to their instinct and are unaccustomed to thinking. Anatomically, an animal's center of sensitivity or judgment is not as highly developed as that of man. This is why animals are exploited all their lives by men and finally killed to be eaten.

Those who eat animal products are in a similar manner exploited and often killed by others, for others or by themselves.

Incidentally, we know of no animal that mobilizes its sons and brothers to kill another nation of creatures as man does. On this point man is insane: his judgment is lower than that of animals.

All men who eat hemoglobinic products depend for sustenance upon animals whose judgment is low and simple. Yet, those of them who become villains, murderers, liars or cowards as a result are not to be blamed or punished. They do not realize that their unhappiness is caused by wrong eating and drinking.

The fault lies with education, the professional variety, that makes man a phonographic parrot instead of a thinking reed.[20]

In the primary school, ideally speaking, a child should learn to be independent, to think, judge and act by and for himself. Such training, however, is quite useless if the child does not have a well-developed brain. It is as useless as trying to teach mathematics or reading to a crocodile. (Its activity is governed by only the lowest judgment, blind and physical — the conditioned reflex.)

Pavlov erred in trying to picture man as merely a machine made up of conditioned reflexes, for the human being has at least six judging abilities that are on a higher level:

1. blind judgment (conditioned reflex)
2. sensory
3. sentimental
4. intellectual
5. social
6. ideological
7. supreme

It is by the fifth judgment, for example, that man commits suicide after killing the lover who has betrayed him. When we pardon the worst criminal, it is the result of the seventh or supreme judgment.

There are some insatiable individuals who seek money,

power, reputation and honor throughout life at all cost. In appearance, they generally have a small skull and a large jaw, the brain being less developed than the mouth or jaw. They are men of action and not of thought. Lynching exists in places where many people have this physiognomical characteristic, where the consumption of animal products is large and where the climate is yang (hot). Yet this very lynching can become a thing of the past if these people will make animal products a less important part of their diet. Education alone is of no use since the problem is physiological in nature. A change in diet is most necessary. We can cite the example of Gandhi as an illustration. If he had not completely given up all animal products during his school days in England, he would have become a very cruel revolutionary.

You have understood, I hope, that it is not only the shape of the head that determines one's behavior. Its contents, its composition and what nourishes it are most important.

You can control your own behavior by controlling your eating and drinking. You can be your own master or a slave of animal judgment. The person whose basic constitution is very yin may murder his mate as a result of too much yin food. He can be more murderously cruel than the yang murderer. Those who eat too much yin food, like the fruitarians or vegetarians of India, are capable of causing great tragedy — the endless splitting of nations.

In the final analysis, however, there is no need to fear animal products. All depends upon quantity, for quantity changes quality. Anything agreeable becomes disagreeable in excess; the desirable becomes undesirable, even hateful, in immoderate quantities.

Here one can learn the superiority of dialectics as opposed to formal logic. The fundamental principles of Occidental logic, the basis of thinking and science in the West, are too rigid and simple for the Oriental. This is why Professor Northrop, author of the interesting book *The Meeting of East and West*, was so astonished at the Oriental mentality.[21]

You must come to understand that in a given situation, the same result can be produced by two antagonistic factors while two opposite results can be produced by different quantities of the same factor.[22]

If you know the macrobiotic cuisine and its dialectical philosophy, you can yinnize or neutralize food that is too yang (animal products) and avoid the fatal domination of lower judgment (cruel, violent, slavish, delinquent) over higher thinking.

Since you are neither accustomed to pure macrobiotic eating nor in haste to reach satori or infinity, the kingdom of heaven, you may occasionally eat dishes made with animal products provided that the recipes are designed to establish a good balance in your organism by neutralizing too much yang and yin (the greatest poison). They are permitted, however, only if they are not contaminated by DDT or other insecticides.

Fish

401. Koi-Koku (Carp Soup)

Carefully remove only the bitter part (gallbladder) of 1 carp. Do not remove scales however. Cut up fish into 1-inch thick slices. Heat 1 tablespoon oil in a pan and sauté shredded burdock root (3 times the volume, after cutting, as carp). Add carp; a bag of used bancha tea twigs and leaves, tied in a cotton bag; and enough water to cover. Simmer for 3 hours. If the water evaporates, add more little by little. When the bones are soft, take out the bag of tea leaves and pour 3 heaping table-spoons of miso diluted in a little water over the carp. Simmer for another hour.

This preparation is good for inflammations and fever and is especially effective for nursing mothers (if there is insufficient milk, they should consume the entire amount in the recipe in 5 days). This is also effective for middle ear infections, pneumonia, arthritis, rheumatism, and amoebic dysentery.

402. Red Snapper

Remove scales and clean fish. Sprinkle with salt. Coat with flour and fry slowly in deep oil, using medium heat. When crisply done, place fish on platter, pour sauce over it, and serve.

403. Fish Sauce

Thinly slice an onion lengthwise, shred Chinese cabbage, sliver carrots, and break up cauliflower into flowerettes. Sauté in a little oil, one after the other in this order: onion, Chinese cabbage, cauliflower, and carrots, stirring well. Season with salt. Add a little water and simmer until tender. Thicken slightly with kuzu and water. This sauce may be used for fried buckwheat noodles, fried vermicelli, etc.

404. Pompano (or Cavalla)

Wash fish and clean. Sprinkle with salt. Coat with flour and prepare the same way as number 402. Miso cream, etc. go well with this fish.

405. Small Whole Fish

Clean and wash small fish, about 2 inches long, such as lake smelt, trout, or sweetfish. Sprinkle with salt and coat with flour. Fry in oil and serve with soy sauce. This preparation is good for all yin diseases.

406. Fried Oysters

Strain off liquid and sprinkle with a little salt. Coat with flour, dip into beaten egg, and coat with bread crumbs. Fry in deep oil.

407. Fried Red Snapper

Slice red snapper into large pieces and sprinkle with salt. Coat the snapper with flavor (a beaten egg and bread crumbs in that order) and fry in oil. Serve with sautéed watercress, cabbage, slivered carrot, etc. seasoned with salt. Mackerel, bonita, yellow tail sardine, etc. are fried in the same way. Serve with grated ginger.

408. Coquilles St. Jacques

Separate flesh from the scallops and wash. Cut into small pieces and sauté with carrots, onions, etc. Place in clam shells and pour on bechamel sauce (number 219). Bake in oven. When prepared without fish, this is permissible for sick people.

409. Shrimp Tempura

Remove shells and sprinkle with salt. Coat with batter and fry. Serve with sauce. To prepare batter: Add a little salt to 1 cup sieved flour. Lightly blend in 2 times as much water. Too much mixing causes sticking and bad results. If glutinous (sweet) rice flour is available, use 20 percent. Add one beaten egg. To prepare sauce: Make stock from kombu and dried bonito flakes and season rather strongly with salt and soy sauce.

Drain the fried shrimp on paper. Place paper doily on a

platter and arrange fried shrimp attractively. Squeeze grated white radish (daikon) lightly with fingers and place on platter. Decorate with parsley and serve. Put sauce in individual small bowls.

410. Red Snapper Tempura

Fillet red snapper, prepare batter as in number 409, dip snapper pieces in batter, and fry.

411. Squid Tempura

Remove skin from squid, score lengthwise and across with a knife, then cut into 1 to 2 inch pieces. Coat with batter as in number 409 and fry. This tempura should be served with vegetable tempura using string beans, watercress, parsley, celery, carrots, etc.

412. Mixed Fried Foods

Use scallops, sliced squid, minced onion, diced carrots, diced abalone, etc. Mix in water, drop by spoonfuls into oil and dry.

413. Egg Tempura

Heat deep oil. Break egg into oil and fry medium.

415. Red Snapper Sashimi

Slice bite-sized pieces of raw red snapper. Arrange 1 row on dish and mound shredded white radish (daikon) and carrot beside and over fish. Then, place another row of fish on top. Serve with grated white radish (daikon) and soy sauce in small dishes.

416. Washed Red Snapper

Fillet red snapper and slice thinly in large slabs. Sprinkle with salt and place in a basket or colander. After 20 minutes run cold water from the faucet over the fish slowly. When the flesh becomes firm, place on a bed of shredded white radish (daikon), carrots, etc. Serve each individual portion with soy sauce and grated ginger in a small dish.

417. Washed Carp

Prepare the same as in number 416. This is very yin and should not be eaten frequently.

418. Loach Soup

Prepare miso soup, adding scallions. Wash loach and add to boiling soup.

419. Yanagawa

Slice loach lengthwise leaving the two sides barely attached. Sauté shredded burdock root in oil and place in a yanagawa pan. Over this lay loach, sliced side up. Pour beaten egg over this. Add sauce that has been rather strongly seasoned with salt and soy sauce and boil. If you do not have a yanagawa pan, use a frying pan, but when serving mound it carefully on a platter so as not to crumble.

420. Broiled or Baked Red Snapper

Clean and scale fish and sprinkle with salt. Bake in oven or cook over gas flame. Fish may be skewered and broiled over fire beautifully. In this case, wrap fins and tail in wet paper. When baking in oven, wipe baking dish with oil. Slice fish into pieces of very large size.

421. Broiled Pompano (Cavallo or Azi)

Scale and clean fish and sprinkle with salt. Broil over flame and serve with soy sauce. Mackerel, pike, sardines, and grey mullet may be prepared in the same way.

422. Barbecued Tuna or Yellowtail

Slice tuna or yellowtail in large pieces and bake in oven. Dip pieces of fish in a half-and-half soy sauce and water mixture and bake again. Remove fish to a platter and pour the soy sauce and water mixture thickened with kuzu flour over it.

423. Red Snapper Stew

Sauté carrots, onions, cabbage, and cauliflower (all cut in large pieces) in oil. Add water and boil well. Cut red snapper into bite-sized pieces and fry crisply in deep oil. Add to vegetables and boil. Fry flour with a little oil until browned and mix with water to form a thin paste. Pour this into fish and vegetable mixture to thicken. Since cauliflower breaks up when cooked too long, it can be boiled separately. Add just before thickening for an attractive dish.

424. Small Red Snapper Nitsuke

Clean and slice fish into chunks, including the head. Boil in half-and-half soy sauce and water mixture.

425. Red Snapper Clear Soup

Prepare stock with 2 quarts of water and 7 to 8 inches of kombu. When the water boils, add 3 tablespoons of dried bonita flakes. Boil well, strain, and put aside. Cut the fish into small pieces. Boil quickly. Boil sliced scallions for an instant. Boil cracknels that have been previously soaked in water. Strain off liquids from separate boilings and add to stock.

Now place some of each ingredient into soup bowls. Season the stock with salt and pour in the bowls. Place a small piece of orange peel into each serving and cover. Chicken, duck, shrimp, white-bait, etc. may be prepared in the same way.

426. Soup Moule

Dice onion and sauté in oil. Add moules (mussels) that have been washed, a small amount of white wine, and a little water and boil over medium heat. When shells open up season with salt.

427. Clam Miso

Remove flesh from large clams. If it is difficult when clams are raw, place them in a pan of water and heat. Wash off sand in water. Sauté minced onion in oil. Thin miso in a little clam juice. Add to onions and stir well. Spoon mixture into shells, place 1 clam along side each, and cover. Broil over grill for a minute and serve.

428. Abalone Nitsuke

Take out abalone from shell and slice into small pieces. Sauté in oil with turnips and carrots and prepare as a nitsuke. Season with salt and soy sauce.

429. Sushi

Slice tuna into thin pieces slightly larger than for raw fish (sashimi). Fry beaten eggs about one-fourth inch thick. Cut into same-sized pieces as tuna and put aside. Boil rice. Mix orange juice with rice and cool. Place 1 heaping tablespoon of the boiled rice in the palm of left hand. Place the first two fingers of the right hand over the rice. Grip and squeeze into cylinder shapes. Place the foregoing ingredients on top of the rice cylinders, one piece to each cylinder and press down with fingers. Arrange attractively on platter. Serve with soy sauce to which a little grated ginger has been added.

430. Hako Sushi

Prepare rice and fish as in number 429. Slice lotus root thinly and prepare in nitsuke style. Sliver carrots and prepare in nitsuke style. Wet rectangular mold with water and arrange fish, fried egg, vegetables, etc. attractively. Cover this with about one-and-one-fourth inches of rice. Press down. Invert over platter and remove mold. Slice into rectangular pieces. Place on individual small dishes. Serve with soy sauce. Hako sushi may be served in individual bowls without molding.

Desserts

501. Karinto

Mix 2 cups flour, 2 tablespoons sesame seeds, a dash of salt, and 1 teaspoon cinnamon. Knead with water into a soft dough. Roll out thin and cut into rectangular strips. Fry until crisp. This can be cut into various decorative shapes (round, large, small), or when rectangular make a slit in the center and push one end through the slit.

502. Polenta Karinto

Prepare as in number 501 using equal parts of flour and polenta (corn flour).

503. Buckwheat Karinto

Prepare as in number 501 using buckwheat flour. This is very good as an in-between meal snack for sick people.

504. Millet Flour Karinto

Mix millet flour and wheat flour in equal parts. Add hazel or cashew nuts cut into small pieces. Add minced orange peel and knead with water. Shape into 3-inch sticks and then slice as thin as possible. Fry in deep oil. Buckwheat flour, rice flour, polenta, etc. may be used and nuts, peanuts, raisins, etc. may be added in small amounts.

505. Ohsawa Bread

Mix 4 parts flour, 2 parts polenta, 2 parts chestnut flour, and 2 parts buckwheat flour. Add a little oil and some raisins. Knead gently with water. Oil pans, fill with a little dough, brush with egg, and bake in oven. For sick people mix buckwheat flour, wheat flour, polenta, millet flour, etc., without chestnuts or raisins. Because no baking powder is used, this bread will not be soft and light, but it is tasty when chewed well.

506. Apple Pie

Slice apples, add a little salt, and cook until tender. Prepare pie dough (see number 89) for crust, line pie plate, fill with apples, and bake.

507. Baked Apples I

Core medium-sized baking apples from the stem. Be careful not to break through the bottom. Fill apples with tahini and salt mixture. Bake in oven until done.

508. Baked Apples II

Prepare pie dough (see number 89) and roll out thin. Cut into pieces large enough to wrap an apple. Prepare apples as in number 507. Place on pieces of dough and wrap; pinch on top to close. Brush with egg yolk and bake. Pie dough may be cut into strips and used to decorate. If apples are too large, they may be cut in quarters but whole apples are more delicious.

509. Chausson

Prepare pie dough (see number 89) and roll out thin. Cut into round pieces about 4 inches in diameter. Use 2 layers together and fold in half, filling with apple jam. Brush with egg yolk and bake in oven.

510. Gateau au Raisin

Prepare pie dough (see number 89) and roll out thinly. Cut in round pieces about 2 inches in diameter. Fill with a few raisins, pinch with thumb and first two fingers to seal. Brush with egg yolk and bake. For variety, fill with cashews.

Variation 1: Wrap 1 layer of thinly rolled pie dough around a stick as thick as a man's thumb. Fry in deep oil, cool, and pull out stick. Fill with apple jam, chestnut jam, pumpkin purée, etc.

Variation 2: Cut pie dough into strips about one-and-one-half inches wide and 4 inches long. Wrap strip around cone-shaped stick about 2 inches thick at one end and about the thickness of a thin pencil at the other. Bake in oven. Cool and remove stick. Fill with apple or chestnut jam or pumpkin purée, etc.

Crackers and Others

511. Crackers

Mix flour with oil, salt, and water and knead. Roll out and cut into 2-inch squares. Make small dots with chopsticks and bake in oven. Crackers can be made from buckwheat flour, oatmeal, polenta, etc. Biscuits can be made by rolling dough out thicker. season with spices as desired.

512. Halawah

Brown 1 cup semoule (coarse wheat flour) in 4 tablespoons oil. Add 2 tablespoons raisins, and 1 apple chopped. Mix with 4 times as much water, 1 teaspoon of salt, and cook together over low heat. When thickened add 2 teaspoons of cinnamon. Wet baking dish with cold water. Line bottom with some minced parsley, and pour mixture over it. Chill. Invert over platter and serve. Chestnut flour, mashed boiled chestnuts, or mashed boiled pumpkin can be poured in alternate layers with above mixture. A tube mold or round mold may be used as desired.

513. Semoule

Prepare as in number 512 using only coarsely ground whole grain flour browned in a little oil. This can be used as a staple food.

514. Sandwiches

Nitsuke vegetables of different varieties, pumpkin cream, chestnut cream, apple jam, etc. used as filling between thin slices of bread make interesting sandwiches. Best for sick people are those made with Ohsawa bread using grain only and spreads made of vegetables only. Chapati, crepes, etc. may also be used for sandwiches.

515. Canapes

Spread a variety of food on small bread squares. Bake these in the oven for a short time.

CHAPTER 9

Yin-Yang Theory

Yin and yang are antagonistic but complementary forces. This statement is already incomprehensible to most Occidentals, according to my experience. I have, therefore, simplified the theory that underlies it in this guidebook. Until your comprehension of our philosophy deepens, follow my directions completely, strictly, and without fear. In your moments of uncertainty be resolved to see the matter through to its happy ending, in the manner that Professor Herrigel followed the master Awa.[23] It is less difficult than fasting.

Remember, you may eat as much as you like as long as you chew very well.

You have the right and the responsibility to pursue health and happiness but it must be done by you for yourself, without depending on others. In this you are but following the example set by all wild animals.

Here is a short outline of the yin-yang theory:

According to our philosophy, there is nothing but yin and yang in the world. yin and yang, physically speaking, are centrifugal and centripetal force, respectively, Centrifugal force is expansive; it produces silence, calmness, cold and darkness. Centripetal force, on the other hand is constrictive and produces sound, action, heat and light in turn.

The following physical phenomena are consequences of

these two fundamental forces:

	Yin	Yang
Tendency	expansion	contraction
Position	outward	inward
Structure	space	time
Direction	ascent (up)	descent (down)
Color	purple	red
Temperature	cold	hot
Weight	light	heavy
Factor	water	fire
Atomic	electron	proton
Element	potassium (K) - the representative yin element. All elements in the periodic table (O, P, Ca, N, etc.) are yin excepting the few listed in the next column as yang.	sodium (Na) - the representative yang element. The yang elements in the periodic table are: H, As, C, Li, Na, Mg.

Biological and Physiological

	Yin	Yang
Biological	vegetable	animal
Agricultural	salad	cereal
Sex	female	male
Nervous System	sympathetic	para-sympathetic
Birth	cold season	hot season
Movement	feminine	masculine
Taste	sweet, sour, hot (curry)	salty, bitter
Vitamins	C	A, D, K

Bio-ecology

	Yin	**Yang**
Country of Origin	tropical	frigid
Season	growth in summer	growth in winter

What should we eat? Which is better, to be a fruitarian or a vegetarian? Are they both bad?

Study these questions. Think, think and think some more. Thinking alone will give you understanding, health and happiness.

True thinking is done in yin and yang terms — practical dialectics, the key to the kingdom of heaven.

For the person who knows and can balance the forces of yin and yang, the universe and life are the greatest free university available to man. For the individual who knows nothing about yin-yang, life is Hell on earth.

Macrobiotic Table of Foods

Attention:

Only the foods in the cereal category are meant to be used as principal foods. They can be eaten daily and at every meal. They form the foundation of the macrobiotic way of eating.

All other food and drink listed, whether yin or yang, is to be used in small quantities, occasionally and with care. For example: Apple, although it is listed as the most yang fruit cannot be safely eaten as often as whole brown rice. Even though apples are yang, the whole category of fruit is a very yin one as compared to the cereal category. Therefore, only a small quantity of apple is occasionally eaten by those who are well. No fruit at all should be eaten by those who are ill.

The food and drink categories themselves, e.g. cereals, vegetables, etc., are in an order that designates the quantity to be used (percentage of total food served) and the frequency with which they are used. For example:

Cereals are always used as the basis for a meal. They are used in the greatest quantity — at least sixty percent of the total amount of food served.

Vegetables are used to supplement the cereals but in lesser quantities and less frequently.

Fish is used in even smaller amounts and even less often.

Animal products, dairy products, fruits and the miscellaneous foods listed are again used in successively lesser amounts and much less often.

All drinks, whether yin or yang on the list, are to be used in the smallest quantity of all and the least often. If possible, take only a total of eight ounces of liquid per day. [See the discussion of less liquids beginning on page 53. -ed.]

It is further advisable to choose foods that are at or reasonably near the midpoint between extreme yin and extreme yang within each category, unless there is a specific reason for another choice. This is the delicate balance point at which the greatest health and happiness can be achieved.

We cannot over-emphasize the point that macrobiotic living is not rigid adherence to a set of rules. The maintenance of a healthy balance in our daily lives demands from each individual an adaptability and an awareness of the constantly changing influences of many factors. This makes happy and healthy existence a full time job.

The type of climate one lives in and the sort of activity one is engaged in determine what and how one eats. (Factors such as place of birth, the type of constitution one has, the season of the year, as well as many other things are taken into consideration as one's comprehension of the order of the universe grows.) For instance, the man who lives in a cold climate needs foods that are slightly more yang than those necessary for one who inhabits the tropics, while the person who works in the fields can tolerate slightly more yin food than can he whose work confines him to a desk. Everything is relative to and is determined by the individual himself, for no set of rules can possibly cover all the variations that exist from one person to the next.

The phrase "more yang" should not be construed to mean a diet based wholly on meat, just as "more yin" does not imply meals that are made up of mostly fruits and sugar. The fact that one's daily intake of food is based preponderantly on grains, however, is taken for granted.

There is yin and yang in everything. Take rice for example. Basically, whole grain brown rice is more yang than polished white rice. However, among the various varieties of brown rice there are some that are more yin or yang than others. A final determination is dependent upon at least three factors:

> How was the rice cultivated?
> In what climate?
> What is its size, shape, water content, color?

What is revealed as being of prime importance is the realization that in order to achieve a high degree of health and happiness, an individual should:

1. understand through study the order of the universe of which he is a part;

2. learn to be highly aware of himself and his reactions to his environment;

3. think, think and think all of the time.

Macrobiotic Table of Foods and Beverages
(Listed within each category in order from Yin to Yang)

1. CEREALS

1 yin	corn			kale
	rye			radish
	barley			garlic
	oats			onion
	cracked wheat			parsley
	wheat		2 yang	Hokkaido pumpkin
	millet			carrot
1 yang	rice (whole, brown)			coltsfoot
2 yang	buckwheat			burdock
				cress

2. VEGETABLES

watercress

dandelion (root)

3 yang   jinenjo potato

3 yin	eggplant
	tomato
	sweet potato
	potato
	shiitake mushroom
	pimento
	beans (except azuki)
	cucumber
	asparagus
	spinach
	artichoke
	bamboo sprout
	mushroom
2 yin	green pea
	celery
	lentil
1 yin	purple cabbage
	beet
	white cabbage
1 yang	dandelion (leaf and stem)
	lettuce
	endive

3. FISH

1 yin	oyster
	clam
	octopus
	eel
	carp
	moule (mussel)
	halibut
	lobster
	trout
	sole
1 yang	salmon
	shrimp
	herring
	sardine
	red snapper (tai)
2 yang	caviar

4. ANIMAL PRODUCTS

2 yin	snail

	frog			cashew
--------	-------------------		--------	------------
	pork			hazel nut
	beef		1 yin	olive
	horsemeat		1 yang	strawberry
	hare			chestnut
1 yin	chicken[24]			cherry
1 yang	pigeon		2 yang	apple
	partridge[24]
	duck
	turkey[24]
2 yang	egg[25]
3 yang	pheasant[24]

7. MISCELLANEOUS

3 yin	honey
	molasses
	margarine
2 yin	coconut oil

5. DIARY PRODUCTS

3 yin	yogurt
	sour cream
	sweet cream
	cream cheese
	butter
2 yin	milk
	camembert
	gruyere
1 yang	roquefort
	Edam cheese (Dutch)
2 yang	goat milk

	peanut oil
	corn oil
	olive oil
1 yin	sunflower oil
	sesame oil
	corza oil
	safflower oil
	Egoma oil (made from most Yang sesame seeds)

8. BEVERAGES

3 yin	those containing sugar substitutes
	tea (containing dye)
	coffee
	fruit juice
	all sugared drinks
	champagne
	wine
2 yin	beer
1 yin	mineral water
	soda (carbonated water)
	water (deep well)
	thyme
	menthol

6. FRUITS

3 yin	pineapple
	papaya
	mango
	grapefruit
	orange
	banana
	fig
	pear
2 yin	peach
	lime
	melon
	almond
	peanut

1 yang	armoise (mugwort, yomogi)		kokkoh (creamed, blended cereal drink)
	bancha (common, undyed Japanese tea)	2 yang	mu tea
			haru tea
	chicory		dragon tea
	Ohsawa coffee (yan-noh)		yang yang tea
		3 yang	ginseng root

Remarks

All the listed foods and beverages have been included in order to help in understanding yin and yang. [Originally, there were symbols indicating relative degrees of yin and yang and these have been replaced with "1 yang," "2 yang," etc. -ed.] Any foods used in a macrobiotic diet must be natural, never artificially or industrially prepared. Chicken, turkey or duck that has been chemically fed as well as the eggs from such fowl, are to be avoided.

Fertilized eggs (those that will produce baby chicks) are laid by a hen only after she has been fertilized by a rooster, yet she can and does lay eggs completely on her own. These eggs are non-fertilized eggs, the variety found in most markets and used by the majority of people today. They are lifeless, biologically speaking, and are not used in the macrobiotic diet. The fertilized egg can be recognized by its small size and its shape — rounded at one end and pointed at the other.

Today, it is very difficult to obtain water, salt or even air in its natural, unadulterated form. Fortunately, however, we can resist whatever poisons they have picked up as a result of commercialization and industrialization once the health of our constitution is re-established.

Yin and yang vary according to the climate of origin and

the season of the year. Further, the yin and yang characteristics of food can be greatly influenced by preparation and manner of eating. This is why cooking and table manners are so important. (In old Japan, eating and drinking were considered to be ceremonies of paramount importance — the creation of life and thinking.)

Bear in mind that the invention of fire (without which we could not cook) has a very deep meaning: it marks the point at which the path of man diverged from that of all other animals.

Menu for One Week

Here is one seven-day menu — there are hundreds of other combinations possible.

BREAKFAST	LUNCH	SUPPER
rice cream	whole rice or bread, nitsuke (carrot, radish)	chapati, Russian soup
oat cream	kasha, nitsuke (watercress)	kitune buckwheat noodles
buckwheat cream	rice gomoku (mixed with vegetables)	polenta soup
rice cream	whole rice, misoni (carrot, onion)	soup Jardinier Ohsawa bread
whole bread w/miso, Ohsawa coffee	whole rice, tempura w/tamari	mori (buckwheat)
oat cream	fried rice, nitsuke (carrot)	pumpkin potage, whole bread
none	fried buckwheat, whole bread, Ohsawa coffee	whole rice, oden

Gomashio and natural soy sauce may be used with all foods.

Sho-ban (311) is recommended before or after meals.

Mu tea is for those who have the need to yangize as quickly as possible. Drink it at or between meals. Use it with care: remember that quantity can destroy quality.

Natural soy sauce, miso, tekka or miso cream should be used every day in place of butter, cheese or margarine.

Editor's Note to the Third Edition
by Shayne Oles Suehle

The following suggestions regarding dietary treatment of disease are the personal conclusions of Georges Ohsawa after 50 years of study and experiment. They are, in the opinion of the editor, to be read as one individual's free expression of his views — not as medical prescriptions. The emphasis of Ohsawa's life-work has been to expound the intimate relationship between food and health, a view now supported by an increasingly larger number of scientific researchers. It must be obvious to the reader that a diagnosed disease that has progressed, primarily through a lifetime of inadequate nutrition, to a point beyond cure cannot be reversed by the simple expedient of a diet.

To those young readers who have not yet established an erroneous eating pattern, Ohsawa's work should prove to be an invaluable guide toward future health. To those beyond this point of age, correct nutritional maintenance is the best insurance we can conceive of for future health.

The editor urges upon all students of macrobiotics continued re-readings of Ohsawa's works, with the ultimate aim of developing the highest personal integration between good health, good nutrition and good judgment.

CHAPTER 10

Suggestions For Macrobiotic Treatment of Disease Symptoms

After studying the yin-yang theory beginning on page 110, you have by now selected one of the ten ways of eating to re-establish your health and happiness.

Diet No. 7 is certainly the easiest and most direct way. In this case, no other specific treatment is necessary. After your recovery you can use any of the foods and beverages listed in the table on page 115.

If you want to hasten the improvement during your initial macrobiotic practice, read the following suggestions and choose what is helpful to you.

[Currently the best book on macrobiotic healing methods is Cornellia and Herman Aihara's *Natural Healing from Head to Toe*, which is highly recommended to those interested in greater understanding of macrobiotic thinking or to those needing specific suggestions for any disease. -ed.]

General Suggestions

Amebic Dysentery: See **Parasites**.

Anemia: Strict observance of Diet No. 7 with tekka no. 1 (210). Drink less.

Cold: Kuzu drink (317), ume-sho-kuzu drink (325), special rice cream drink (326).

Cough: Kohren tea (316) or renkon (lotus) tea (318). **External**: ginger compress (801), albi plaster (802).

Diarrhea: Kuzu drink (317), ume-sho-kuzu drink (325). **External**: ginger compress (801) or konnyaku compress (810); ginger hip bath (808).

Dysentery: See **Diarrhea**.

Eczema: Strict observance of Diet No. 7. Drink as little as possible. Nothing else.

Fever: Kuzu drink (317), ume-sho-kuzu drink (325), rice potage (23), special rice cream drink (326). **External**: chlorophyll plaster (813), tofu plaster (803), soybean plaster (811), carp plaster (812).

General Weakness: See **Anemia**.

Inflammation: Ginger compress (801) followed by albi plaster (802), tofu plaster (803), or chlorophyll plaster (813).

Paralysis: Strict observance of Diet No. 7. Drink as little as possible. Nitsuke made from watercress (65), dandelion (163), or thistle (azami) are particularly effective. See *The First Macrobiotic Cookbook* for additional recipes.

Parasites: Mugwort tea (306), raw whole rice (48a; one handful in place of breakfast). Observe Diet No. 7 very strictly plus gomashio (50), umeboshi (51), or a handful of Hokkaido pumpkin seeds (49).

Swelling: Radish drink no. 2 (321), azuki juice (319).

Whooping Cough: See **Cough.**

Wounds: See **Eczema.**

There is an endless variety of diseases known to man, all very complicated and all very difficult to diagnose even for doctors equipped with the latest modern devices that increase in number day by day. Each disease is accompanied, however, by one or another of the above symptoms: sometimes they are combined. If you are observing one of the ways of macrobiotic eating and drinking (Diets No. 5, 6, or 7) you can care for yourself according to the preceding advice and the following symptomatic suggestions.

Macrobiotic External Treatment

801. Ginger Compress

Use 4 ounces raw ginger (crushed or grated) or one heaping teaspoonful dried ginger powder. Place in cotton sack. Boil one-half to one gallon water. Turn off flame. Drop sack into water. When water turns pale yellow, squeeze towel in it. Cover painful part. (Liquid should be as hot as possible.) Cover compress with large towel to prevent rapid cooling. Cover skin with one nylon sheet, apply compress and cover it with another nylon sheet to retard cooling even longer. Change compress three or four times during fifteen minutes.

802. Albi Plaster

Albi is the Indian name for the root used in this treatment. It is called yutia in America, sato-imo in Japan, and taro in Africa.

Crush albi very carefully. Add an equal amount of wheat

flour, and more flour if the mixture is too wet. Add ten percent raw grated ginger. Spread mixture on sheet of cloth, paper, or nylon to a thickness of one-half inch. Apply plaster to painful area, cover with nylon sheet. Leave on several hours. Apply only after a ginger compress, up to 4 or 5 per day.

803. Tofu Plaster

Squeeze liquid out of tofu (white soybean "cheese") and add ten percent wheat flour. Spread this directly on any area that is painful or inflamed. All pain, fever or inflammation will soon be relieved.

804. Sesame Ginger Juice

Thoroughly mix one teaspoonful sesame oil and one teaspoon ginger juice. Apply to affected areas. Very good for headache; stops dandruff and falling of hair.

805. Pure Sesame Oil

Filter sesame oil through cotton or gauze. Apply one drop in each eye before sleep. Do not be alarmed if there is temporary smarting. Good for all eye disease.

806. Chlorophyll Hip Bath

Cook two or three dried leaves (hiba) of Japanese white radish plus a handful of salt in one gallon of water. Sit in tub filled with enough hot water to cover vital areas. Add cooked mixture at intervals so that bath will remain strong and hot. Take this bath 15 to 20 minutes before going to bed and drink a cup of sho-ban (311) immediately after taking the bath. This hip bath is very good for all female sexual organ diseases.

807. Salt Hip Bath

Make number 806 with salt alone, no radish leaves.

808. Ginger Hip Bath

Crush one pound of ginger. Place in cotton sack and boil in two gallons of water. Very good for violent dysentery: If not too extreme, make half the quantity, squeeze towel in solution, and apply as a compress on the abdomen.

809. Salt Compress

Heat two or three pounds of salt. Place in cotton sack. Apply to painful area.

810. Konnyaku Compress

Boil two or three pounds konnyaku (paste made from powdered Japanese tuberose). Apply this, wrapped in two towels, to painful area.

811. Soybean Plaster

Soak one cup of soybeans in five cups of water for twenty-four hours. Crush, add 10 percent wheat flour. Apply on forehead for fever or on any inflamed area. It absorbs fever miraculously.

812. Carp Plaster

Take a one-pound carp, cut off head and catch blood in a cup. A patient suffering acute pneumonia should drink this liquid before it coagulates. Crush the remainder of the fish, place in cloth and apply to the chest. Measure temperature every thirty minutes. When it returns to normal (within five or six hours) remove plaster.

Many people have been cured by this treatment after having tried antibiotics in vain.

813. Chlorophyll Plaster

Crush watercress, spinach or large leaves of any vegetable. Spread on piece of cloth and apply to forehead to absorb fever.

814. Tea Compress

Grill bancha tea (toast until dark brown in frying pan) and prepare as for drinking. Add five percent salt. Soak cloth in this solution and apply to eye for ten to fifteen minutes, three times a day. Good for all eye diseases.

815. Dentie

This is prepared from the head of eggplant, preserved in salt, dried and finally burned. The ashes are mixed with salt, finely ground and used as a tooth powder. Can be applied to a painful tooth. The pain will be instantly relieved. If you are suffering from pyorrhea, brush your teeth with dentie and apply it to your gums (the outer side only) before going to bed every night.

816. Rice Plaster

Crush whole raw rice. Add a small amount of water. Apply this directly to a painful wound.

Specific Dietary Suggestions for Disease

Do not forget that the following specific, symptomatic directions are not necessary if you are following Diet No. 7 or if your case is not critical. You will see improvement by simply observing the macrobiotic way (Diet No. 6 or 7) without the help of others or of any device or medicine — on your own. You will have discovered the real meaning of prayer and fasting.

If your recovery is slow, you have lost faith in God, the Creator of the infinite universe. You have replaced it with faith in something that is a substitute for God, like Science-the-Creator or another new religion, mysticism, spiritualism, conceptualism, social reform or superstition.

Real prayer is not begging or supplication. Rather it is deep and continuing meditation on the structure of the infinite universe (the kingdom of heaven and its Justice).

True fasting is not detachment from all eating and drinking. On the contrary, it is strict and absolute attachment to that only which is absolutely necessary to sustain life.

You cannot detach yourself from air, water and light, the synthesis of which are the cereals that form the true foundation of our very existence. The use of cereal, fire and salt distinguishes man, his civilization and his culture from all other living things. Without recognition of this basic fact, he is lost in his quest for well-being. And, he has failed to recognize it. He has come very far along the path of giving up the principle of life, his Mother, and of seeking only sensory pleasures. The resultant, complicated way of living produces all kinds of difficulties and unhappiness.

Give up everything that is not absolutely necessary to your life for at least a week or two. You will catch a glimpse of freedom, happiness and justice. You may soon understand why macrobiotic persons are completely immunized from disease. The decision is yours.

Air Sickness

Drink as little as possible before flying. Keep some gomashio (50) in your mouth while in the air. No sugar or sweets. No alcohol. Seasickness is treated the same way. Note: If you observe macrobiotic directions for more than one or two months, you will never be seasick or airsick. Incidentally, pregnant women who are macrobiotic do not suffer from morning sickness.

Apoplexy

You will never have this illness if you are macrobiotic. The best food for those who have been stricken is Diet No. 7.

Appendicitis

No macrobiotic person can be a victim of this illness. Diet No. 7 is best. **External**: Ginger compress (801) followed by albi plaster (802).

Arthritis

Very easy to cure along with all other so-called incurable diseases. Observe Diet No. 7 very strictly. Apply ginger compress (801) followed by albi plaster (802).

Basedow's Disease

Easy to cure with Diet No. 7 and gomashio (50).

Bed-wetting

Stop taking anything rich in vitamin C, potassium or phosphorus. No water, juices, potato, tomato, eggplant, orange or grapefruit. Take Diet No. 7 with a little gomashio (50). You can cure this in ten to twenty hours. After having been cured, try one potato, tomato, orange or any sugared pie or pudding. You will suffer an almost immediate recurrence.

Burns

Diet No. 7. Drink no water at all for a few days. Apply sesame oil. Umeboshi (51) are very useful (one or two per day).

Cancer

This is a most interesting malady. It is, along with heart and mental disease, one of the three most destructive scourges of our time, a striking illustration of the ineffectiveness of modern symptomatic medicine.

Lack of understanding of the structure of the infinite universe and its order makes it impossible for modern medicine to cure even an insignificant wart, and what is more important, to prevent its occurrence in the first place. All symptomatic treatment is analytical and consequently prohibitive, negative and destructive. For example, it attempts to lower fever without knowing the origin and mechanism of that fever; it uses alkalines against pyrosis (over-acidity) when it can be cured easily by eliminating the intake of acid-producing food; it uses antibiotics against all microbial diseases without eliminating that which makes microbes dangerous; finally, it destroys suffering organs through surgery without dealing with the real cause of disease: man's faulty judgment in eating and drinking.

Cancer, mental disease and cardiac ailments are simply the result, the dead-end of symptomatic medicine which does not comprehend the life process itself. Cancer is the most extreme yin disease.

So-called incurable diseases attack those who have a strong constitution by birth or the false resistance given by symptomatic treatment.

No illness is more simple to cure than cancer (including mental disease and heart trouble) through a return to the most elementary and natural eating and drinking: Diet No. 7.

If you have no faith in the teaching of Jesus (prayer and fasting) try a ginger compress (801) followed by an albi plaster (802).

Cataract

Caused by the use of too much sugar and vitamin C over a long period of time. Diet No. 7 with gomashio (50).

Children's Dysentery

Caused by too much vitamin C and fruit. Diet No. 7, treatment: kuzu drink (317), ume-sho-kuzu drink (325), ginger compress (801), and ginger hip bath (808).

Congestion

Ginger compress (801) followed by albi plaster (802).

Constipation

Caused by eating too much food that is rich in yin elements such as sugar, vitamin C, salad, fruits, potato, eggplant, tomato (see Table of Foods, page 115). Eliminate these and you will be cured as if you had awakened from a nightmare.

If you are not cured rapidly by eating Diet No. 7, your case is very serious. Your intestines, the root of your life, are paralyzed and without elasticity. Be patient for a few days, if not weeks, without worrying. As long as you have an anus and you are eating, you need have no fear: that which has a beginning has an end. Natural evacuation will begin as soon as your intestines have re-established their original elasticity. Meanwhile, no poisonous fermentation will be produced in your intestines by the natural, macrobiotic food you are taking.

Cough

This includes whooping cough, tuberculosis and asthmatic coughs. Follow Diet No. 7 with a little gomashio (50). Any cough can be stopped in a few days, even a twenty-year-old asthmatic cough. Refer to General Suggestions, page 121 and use dragon tea (314) and kohren tea (316).

Cramps

Caused by too much yin food or drink, especially fruits and sweets. They attack, first of all, the legs (the most yang parts of the body) which can ordinarily neutralize too much yin. If they attack the heart, it is fatal.

All symptoms and suffering are alarm signals given by God. If you destroy such signals by using symptomatic treatment or sedation, you leave yourself completely unprotected.

Dandruff

See Falling of Hair, page 133. Dandruff is the first step toward mental disease.

Detachment of Retina

Diet No. 7 with no liquid at all for a few days. You and your doctor will be surprised by a natural cure. You, yourself, must discover the mechanism of this extremely simple cure if you wish to live a joyful, happy and interesting life. You will be surprised when you understand through study why symptomatic medicine cannot cure such a simple malady.

Diabetes

Caused by too much yin food and drinking. No doctor can cure diabetes even thirty years after the discovery of insulin; the number of victims, increases day by day. In fact, in the

United States alone, there are millions who suffer from this disease. This illustrates the limit of scientific, symptomatic medicine. Why not go back to the medicine of Jesus in this country of Christianity? So-called incurable diabetes can be cured within ten days if the diseased person can really understand the meaning of prayer and fasting, the structure of the infinite universe, and if he has a strong will. Otherwise, he will feed doctors and the pharmaceutical industry as long as he lives. He has no need to go to Hell after death for he is there already.

The best way to cure this disease is Diet No. 7 with one hundred grams of potimarron (the nickname for a variety of pumpkin grown in Hokkaido, Japan) cooked with fifty grams of azuki (red beans from the same area) daily. Both of these foods can be cultivated in America and Canada or wherever conditions are similar to those in cold Hokkaido. I have cultivated them successfully in Belgium.

Potimarron and azuki are very rich in carbohydrates or glucose, both prohibited by doctors for diabetic patients. Yet, it is curious that rice, potimarron and azuki can cure diabetes easily and completely without drugs.

Carbohydrates are transformed into sugar in our bodies, so symptomatic medicine prohibits them for fear of aggravating the disease. If, however, diabetes is cured with a non-carbohydrate diet, the cure is not genuine. What results is a negative condition that is violence itself, just as if the patient and his illness were in prison. In such an instance, the disease is iatrogenic.

The fear that dominates symptomatic medicine stems from an ignorance of the structure of the infinite universe, God. How can such a lack of understanding exist in a great, civilized country like the Untied States?

Diarrhea, Dysentery

Do not drink any water. Apply a ginger compress (801) followed by an albi plaster (802) to your abdomen, or use a ginger hip bath (808). Drink kuzu drink (317) or ume-sho-kuzu drink (325).

Eczema

No symptomatic treatment is necessary at all. Diet No. 7 strictly, with as little liquid as possible. All eczema comes from diseased, overworked kidneys.

Epilepsy

No doctor can cure this disease yet Jesus cured it easily by prayer and fasting. My wife has frequently cured this malady within three days. The easiest and quickest way is Diet No. 7 with no liquid for several days.

Falling of Hair, Dandruff and Baldness

Caused by too much yin (Vitamin C, fruits, sugar, salads, anything rich in potassium or phosphorus, too much drinking water, etc.) Stop these and you will be cured without any other treatment. When you are completely cured, try an interesting experiment. Take one of these yin foods, e.g. a pear, some eggplant, tomato, vinegar, or honey before going to bed. You will be shocked to see ten times more fallen hair on your pillow and in your comb than the day before. All cosmetics, dyes, lotions, as well as combs and brushes made of plastic are very yin.

Fear

See Epilepsy.

Glaucoma

Caused by too much yin food, especially fats and alcoholic drinks. Take Diet No. 7. Drink as little liquid as possible.

Gonorrhea

No macrobiotic person can be affected by this or any other venereal disease. Take Diet No 7 with as much gomashio (50) as possible for a week or two. You can take all yang drinks, e.g. rice tea (301), Ohsawa coffee (304), Kokkoh (305), mug-wort tea (306), mu tea (309), sho-ban (311), yang-yang tea (313), dragon tea (314), haru tea (315), umeboshi juice (324), ume-sho-kuzu drink (325).

Headache

This is a warning of incipient cerebral hemorrhage. Caused by food rich in yin elements as mentioned above. If you take a medicine like aspirin to kill the pain, it is suicidal: you are eclipsing your illness by paralyzing your nervous system, the body's first line of defense. All headaches are alarms indicating too much acidity and are the signal of danger penetrating the very headquarters of your life. (Aspirin is a very strong acid as are all vitamins.) Take a spoonful of gomashio (50). The following macrobiotic drinks are very helpful: Ohsawa coffee (304), kokkoh (305), mu tea (309), sho-ban (311), kuzu drink (317), ume-sho-kuzu drink (325), special rice cream drink (326). See Cold, page 122.

Heart Disease

Although millions are being spent each year for research, the mortality rate for heart disease in America is the highest in the world. Western medicine offers neither an effective prevention nor a positive cure. According to our philosophical, cosmological, dialectic, macrobiotic medicine, the multiple factors involved in heart disease are classified in one simple category: YIN. Since the heart is one of the most yang organs in our body, its biggest enemy is yin.

I would have to write a large book to explain the mechanism and the therapeutics of heart disease. It is a very interesting subject but at my age I do not have the time. You will have to learn through study, and write the book for yourselves.

Observe Diet No. 7 if you are in haste. Later, study my publications. Try ransho (322) if your case is very urgent, once a day for three days only. You will be surprised at the improvement that follows.

My fourth book in French, written especially for European doctors and health practitioners, *Guide Pratique de la Medicine d'Extreme-Orient,* explains further.[26]

Hemophilia

This is an extreme yin disease caused by too much yin such as Vitamin C, fruits and salad. Diet No. 7 with as much gomashio (50) as possible.

Hemorrhages

This includes gastric, intestinal, uterine, and nasal bleeding; bleeding gums and bleeding ulcers. All hemorrhages are produced by eating and drinking too much yin. It is very rare that bleeding comes from yang in excess. If this is the case, you need do nothing. It will go away. See all the General Suggestions beginning on page 121.

Hemorrhoids (Piles)

Diet No. 7. If you are suffering severely, try a ginger compress (801) followed by an albi plaster (802).

Hernia

Diet No. 7 with shio kombu (150).

High Blood Pressure

See Heart Disease, pages 134-135.

Hyper-insulinism

This is a transitional disease which terminates in diabetes (hypo-insulinism). You can cure this very easily by using Diet No. 7.

Impotency

Natural, moderate and normal sexual desire is instinctive and a sign of good health. Normal relations for a healthy man and woman imply the sharing of ecstasy once a night until the age of sixty, at least. Macrobiotic persons can enjoy this pleasure until even later in life, possibly to the age of eighty. One of the greatest Buddhist monks of Japan, Rennyo (1415-1499), left a three-year-old child when he died at the age of eighty-four. He had twenty-seven children in all.

Statistically speaking, longevity belongs to the macrobiotic monk, while restaurateurs and doctors die youngest in Japan. It is indeed strange that those who prepare delicious food and those who take care of our health are not only strangers to the secret of life but are its enemies.

Sexual appetite and the hunger for food are of major importance to man as motivating forces. Without the desire for food no man can live a joyful and happy life; without sexual appetite no animal race can survive on earth.

The healthy man is active and the healthy woman is passive in sexual life for the following reasons: man is yang, active, centripetal and strong (in pathological extremes — violent, destructive and cruel); woman is yin , passive, centrifugal and soft (in pathological extremes — weak, negative, exclusive, antisocial and an escapist). By nature, man and woman are antagonistic yet complementary in their behavior and are thus obliged to play tag permanently. That is why life is so thought-provoking, so interesting and so dramatic. Without sexual desire, life is a desert. Unfortunately, there are many individuals who cannot enjoy sexual love. They are asexual because of a yin nature by birth (caused by the mother's faulty diet) or a yin nature acquired by taking too much yin food (sugar, fruits, industrial drinks, etc.).

Man should be yang. If he is yin, he will be very unhappy. If he is too yang and becomes cruel and destructive, never mind. He will finish very young and tragically.

Women are yin by nature. It is when they become yang by taking too much yang food (animal products) that they become unhappy. Some women detest a man's sexual desire. They have taken a great deal of yang food, have become too masculine and have no desire to be loved by a male. They become homosexual or love animals to an extreme degree. At best, they love passive, feminine men who are obedient, docile and kind. Their life is unhappy for it violates the basic principle of existence. At the other extreme, if women are too yin to be loved, so fearful that they flee from any sexuality, they will be sad all through their lives.

Men who are too yin are much more unhappy than those who are too yang. Those women who are too yang are much more unhappy than those who are too yin. Because of such abnormality in their personality and sexual life, they cannot build a happy home. However, a man who is too yin and a woman who is too yang can be less unhappy together than alone.

Almost all of the unhappiness of life in general and of family life in particular comes from sexual difficulties that include impotency, a lack of joyful sexuality or too much pathological sexual activity between man and wife. No person can be happy and productive if his sexual needs are not satisfied in his family environment. In fact, many a great man, such as Socrates, Confucius and Tolstoy have come to a desperate end as the result of having a sick wife. It is interesting to note that some yin men have become famous under the protection of a yang mistress who in turn had a very yin husband: Anatole France and Mme. Caillavet, Nelson and Mrs. Hamilton.

What is the cause of impotency and frigidity in women and the lack of sexual appetite in men? Sexual hormones are a primary factor. Unfortunately, both men and women do not understand that they can control their hormones and establish a healthy appetite for sex by means of correct food. As a result, their lives are full of bitterness and difficulty; they can only play blindman's bluff.

Further, men and women choose a life's companion without having a basis on which to judge who is the best mate among the many available possibilities. Their supreme judging ability is deeply clouded and they are guided by sensory, sentimental, intellectual or economic judgment. The majority are motivated by the lowest judgment of all: blind, physical attraction. With a knowledge of the Unique Principle of the infinite universe, yin-yang, however, they would be able to choose the best mate, and if they failed in their choice, they could transform their partner's biological, physiological and psychological constitution through macrobiotics.

The philosophy of the Orient, the foundation of all science and all technology, forbids boys and girls to play or study in the same room after the age of seven. Biologically and physio-

logically, this is a natural method of strengthening the yang
nature of boys and the yin nature of girls. Furthermore, all
children learn the yin-yang philosophy and its application on
every level of living from the beginning of primary school.
They are taught how to find the best companion for life from a
bio-ecological standpoint. They learn that a future happy
couple should choose one another from among those who
were born on the antipode of the earth's orbit, some one hundred and eighty days apart, and should come from families
that are as different as possible. This makes for the greatest
mutual attraction.[27]

There are, finally, endless varieties of food and drink that
can change our constitutions, sexual desire, intellectual ten-
dencies, social behavior and as a consequence, our society and
destiny. Some are miraculous aphrodisiacs while others are in-
stantaneously effective anti-aphrodisiacs, e.g. shiitake (a variety of Japanese mushroom), kampyo (a cord made from a kind
of pumpkin), konnyaku (a tuber), and especially kuwai (ar-
rowhead) which kills our sexual appetite completely and immediately. Note that these are all vegetables. They are always
used in Buddhist temples and in Japanese religious families.
(Sugar, sweets, juices, ice cream, soft drinks, all fruits but especially those that come from hot countries — potatoes, tomatoes, eggplant, and Vitamin C, can easily substitute for them.)

Some women serve them, appropriately, in the kitchen
when their husbands are too yang (cruel and violent in their
everyday behavior and sexual life). Husbands who are ignorant of the secrets of macrobiotic cooking take these foods continuously and are rendered docile or impotent.

I will not reveal any further secrets here for there are always some who wish to misuse them. It is better to observe
the normal macrobiotic way that transforms your constitution

slowly but steadily.

Food sustains us. Because of it we think, speak, work, love, hate, destroy and create. Though we can easily kill the strongest man by feeding him something very yin, it is much less difficult to kill or strengthen sexual appetite.

Impotent, cold women are generally suspicious, unbelieving, mystical and backbiting in their manner. In time, this tendency develops into insanity. Take Diet No. 7 strictly and absolutely for a few weeks.

Influenza

Whole rice cream (22a), thick kuzu drink (317) ume-sho-kuzu drink (325). If you are suffering severely, mu tea (309) or haru tea (315). See General Suggestions, page 121. No truly macrobiotic person can be attacked by this disease.

Insomnia

Diet No. 7 strictly. Take a cup of sho-ban (311) before going to bed.

Jaundice

Fasting for at least three days is recommended. Later, rice cream (22a) with a diced umeboshi plum (51). If this disease occurs in a baby that is being breast fed and is not cured in a few days, it can be very dangerous. The mother must make herself yang by eating yang food. No treatment is necessary for the baby.

Kidney Diseases

There are so many kidney ailments that I do not have the space to analyze each one individually. In general, remember the kidney is a very yang organ, three times more so than the heart. Therefore, almost all kidney disease comes from eating too much yin food and especially from too many yin drinks. Drink less and less. Avoid all foods that are very yin by consulting the table on page 115. **Specific:** special rice cream drink (326), azuki juice (319) with a pinch of salt. If pain is severe, apply a ginger compress (801) followed by an albi plaster (802).

Leprosy

Like cancer, this is very easy to cure. It attacks only those with a very good constitution by birth. The cause is too much yin (same as cancer). Take Diet No. 7. Drink very, very little. Apply a ginger compress (801) followed by an albi plaster (802).

Leukemia (Cancer of the Blood)

See Cancer, page 129. This can be cured within ten days if you have completely understood the philosophy of Far Eastern medicine and mastered macrobiotic cooking. Try it — you will be amazed.

Leukoderma (White Leprosy)

This is the result of eating too much yin food, mostly fruit. Eliminate the fruit and you will be cured. Generally, those who suffer from this ugly and disagreeable malady are disliked because they are very stubborn. Only as a last resort will they try the macrobiotic way.

Leukorrhea (White, green or yellow)

This is very common. Even rich, clever and beautiful women are unhappy if they have this ailment. The green variety is most yin. Use Diet No. 7. Take a very hot chlorophyll or salt hip bath (806 or 807) fifteen minutes before going to bed for at least two weeks.

Low Blood Pressure
See Heart Disease, pages 134-135.

Meningitis
Diet No. 7 with a little gomashio (50) for a month. After that Diet No. 6, then No. 5, both with any nitsuke (see 61, 62, and 64 through 68.)

Menstrual Irregularity, Pain
Use normal macrobiotic food such as Diet No. 7, 6, or 5. Mu tea (309). Drink less. Take a hip bath (806 or 807).

Migraine
Diet No. 7, 6, or 5 with a little gomashio (50). You will be cured in a few days.

Morning Sickness
No macrobiotic woman suffers from this disease. Drink dragon tea (314) if it is severe.

Myopia
Most types are caused by an increase in the diameter of the eye (a yin condition). Other types of myopia are caused by an increase in the refractive power of the lens (a yang condition). Therefore, myopia can be the result of either too much yin or too much yang food and drink. All types can be cured by the normal macrobiotic diet — a good balance of yin and yang food and drink.

Nephritis
See Kidney diseases, page 140.

Neurasthenia
Diet No. 7 only with a little gomashio (50).

Obesity
Diet No. 7 with thirty to sixty grams of raw radish, plus a little gomashio (50) for one month or more.

Otitis Media (middle ear infection)
Diet No. 7, followed very strictly. Also Russian soup (70). If very severe, eat miso zosui (20) for a few days.

Ozena
This is a nasal discharge caused by ulcerative disease of the mucous membrane. Diet No. 7, strictly and drink as little as possible.

Paranoia
This variety of schizophrenia has an extreme yin basis. Its victim's pathologically excessive tendency to all things yang leads to violence, cruelty and murderous explosiveness. Diet No. 7 is recommended with no yang preparations.

Parkinson's Disease
There are two categories, yin and yang, both of which are not understood by symptomatic medicine. The yin variety manifests itself in slight trembling, while the yang type is very energetic (*Paralysis Agitans*). The first is cured by Diet No. 7 with a little gomashio (50) and less drinking. The second is treated with Diet No. 5 or No. 4 without gomashio and in-

cludes moderate drinking.

Periostitis

Diet No. 7 with a little gomashio (50). Ginger compress (801) followed by albi plaster (802) four times a day.

Peritonitis

Diet No. 7 with small bits of umeboshi plum (51). Ginger compress (801) followed by albi plaster (802) for great pain.

Poliomyelitis (Polio)

This is a very yin sickness. Avoid everything rich in vitamin C, sugar, potassium and acidity. No juices, fruits or salad. Diet No. 7 with a little gomashio (50) plus drinking less and less will be sufficient. Burdock kinpira (63). All yang preparations are good.

Prolapus

Diet No. 7 with a little gomashio (50). Ginger compress (801) followed by albi plaster (802).

Rheumatism

Drink less and less. Take only grilled rice (48b). Use a ginger compress (801) followed by an albi plaster (802).

Schizophrenia

This yin disease is characterized by a separation of mental and physical processes. In most of its forms there is a deficiency of yang (centripetal force), loss of the sense of the boundaries of self, a feeling of unreality. The victim feels out of, away from, and above the earth and his own body. This is the most extreme yin illness of people with basically weak constitutions, just as cancer is the most extreme yin illness of those who have basically strong organisms. Diet No. 7 followed strictly for at least three weeks. Sho-ban (311) and all yang drinks are recommended. (See also, Paranoia).

Sterility
Diet No. 7 strictly for two weeks, then Nos. 6, 5, 4 progressively, for some months. Very hot chlorophyll or salt hip bath (806 or 807) fifteen minutes before going to bed.

Stomachache
Sho-ban (311), ume-sho-kuzu (325) or apply a ginger compress (801) followed by an albi plaster (802). Also, special rice cream drink (326) with a little gomashio (50).

Syphilis
This is contagious only for those who have a yin constitution. It is easy to cure since the spirochete that causes syphilis is very yin, therefore weak and vulnerable to salt. Try Diet No. 7.

Toothache
Apply dentie (815) to tooth or gum. No yin drinking.

Trachoma
Diet No. 7 with a little gomashio (50). Special rice cream drink (326), tekka (210 or 211), and kinpira (63) are especially recommended. Also use a ginger compress (801) followed by an albi plaster (802).

Tuberculosis
Tekka no. 1 (210) is helpful for tuberculosis of the lung

while tekka no. 2 (211) is helpful for tuberculosis of the intestines. [This comment was added by Ohsawa in the margins of the original manuscript. -ed.]

Varicosity

Can be cured rapidly with normal macrobiotic food. Avoid everything yin. A fifteen-minute chlorophyll or salt hip bath (806 or 807) before bed is useful for women.

Wounds

See Burns, page 129.

*   *   *   *   *

Above are the examples of the macrobiotic method of treating common ailments. You should study deeply and learn to treat more complicated illnesses on your own, by and for yourself. Follow the example of animals in the wilderness: be your own doctor. Nothing is impossible if you have faith (a deep comprehension of the structure of the universe and its order). You can even say to the mountain, "Enter into the sea."

CHAPTER 11

Macrobiotic Living

Macrobiotic Food for Infants

The milk of a cow (or of any animal for that matter) is intended for its own offspring, biologically speaking. The human infant should in like manner be nourished by the milk of a human female — for at least nine months but preferably a year. Nursing for this length of time is relatively simple for the macrobiotic woman.

The quality and quantity of its mother's milk controls a baby's destiny since its organism is dependent on this one source of nourishment for its development and well-being. It is therefore, important that the mother understand the philosophy of the Orient and maintain herself in a good nutritional (yin-yang) balance. This is quite easy because the child is the mirror of what mother eats and drinks. Any difficulties that the infant encounters (skin problems, colds, etc.) can be traced directly to liberties that the nursing mother has taken with her diet. The baby's balance will vary according to whether she has had too much yin or too much yang. As such, the breast-feeding woman should ordinarily have no trouble easing her child's difficulty by adjusting the quality and quantity of her own intake.

It goes without saying that breast-feeding (with no other dietary supplements) is best for the baby. But — it is harder on the mother because of the care that she must exercise with her own diet plus the fact that more of her time will be spent in catering to the child's demands. The total effect of nursing on the infant and the mother, however, make it a very worthwhile experience.

For the child who is nursing, cereals and grains may be added to his diet at approximately the age of six months. They should be in an easy-to-take form (cooked a long time and puréed in a blender). Vegetables are added at approximately one year. Diced vegetables cooked in weak miso soup is one way of preparing them. Bear in mind that the ages at which these foods are added are only approximate. You must be flexible. All depends on your judgment and the constitution of your child.

Do not feed a child too much. Moderate hunger, thirst and cold during the first year of life will make your baby yang and will consolidate the foundation of its constitution and personality.

Kokkoh

In cases where mother's milk is not available, you can feed the child with kokkoh (305) according to the directions and the table on page 149.

Preparation of the Bottle

Dilute kokkoh with a volume of fresh water (ten to fifteen parts water to one part kokkoh, according to age). Cook this moderately for twenty minutes. The quantity of the mixture is smaller than that of cow's milk since excessive amounts of water are not to be used.

Schematic Feeding Table for Infants Using Kokkoh
(Macrobiotic Milk)

Age	Kokkoh	Water	Feedings per day	Quantity per feed	Quantity per day
1st day — Some spoonfuls of water with 0.5% salt.					
2nd day	10 gr	100 cc	3 to 5	10 cc	40 cc
3rd day	10 gr	100 cc	5 to 7	20 cc	120 cc
4th day	10 gr	100 cc	5 to 7	30 cc	180 cc
5th day	10 gr	100 cc	5 to 7	40 cc	240 cc
6th day	10 gr	100 cc	5 to 7	50 cc	300 cc
7th day	10 gr	100 cc	5 to 7	60 cc	360 cc
8th day	10 gr	100 cc	5 to 7	70 cc	420 cc
9th day	10 gr	100 cc	5 to 7	80 cc	480 cc
10th day	10 gr	100 cc	5 to 7	90 cc	540 cc
11th day to 30th day	10 gr	100 cc	5 to 7	30 cc	600 cc
2nd month	12 gr	100 cc	6	110 cc	660 cc
3rd month	18 gr	100 cc	6	120 cc	720 cc
4th month	18 gr	100 cc	6	130 cc	780 cc
5th month	18 gr	100 cc	6	140 cc	840 cc
6th month	18 gr	100 cc	5	180 cc	900 cc
7th month	18 gr	100 cc	5	200 cc	1000 cc
8th month	18 gr	100 cc	5	200 cc	1000 cc
9th month	18 gr	100 cc	5	200 cc	1000 cc
10th month to 12th month	18 gr	100 cc	5	200 cc	1000 cc

Do not awaken the baby to feed him. It is better to cancel one bottle if the infant's appetite is not good enough to arouse him in time for his feeding.

Kokkoh is recommended for everyone and may be used as the breakfast for an adult. It can also be used to make a large variety of cakes, drinks and desserts.

In the 4th month, add 5 to 10 grams of purée of onions, carrots, watercress, etc.

In the 5th month, 10 to 50 percent of food can be replaced progressively by whole rice. Cook 1 part rice, 5 to 6 parts water. Continue this to the 9th month.

In the 13th month, give 150 grams of whole rice (cooked with 3 parts water) and 30 to 40 grams cooked vegetables (cooked with a little vegetable oil and salt). Give, also, 2 to 3 cups of water, rice tea (301), or Ohsawa coffee (304).

From the 16th to the 24th month, you can increase the quantity of rice and vegetables progressively, at the rate of 30 grams of rice and 6 grams of vegetables per day.

The General Care of Young Children and Bio-chemical Transmutation

This section is being added to the revised American [third] edition of *Zen macrobiotics* for a very practical reason. The very same adults who have so easily and successfully made macrobiotics their way of life have reacted with fear and uncertainty in the face of the difficulties that can arise when children are introduced to an unfamiliar regimen.

How do we know that we are doing the right thing?

What do we do in the case of . . . ?

Doesn't my child need . . . ?

I have found that I get along well without vitamin C but

what about my growing child?

The questions are endless. Taken together, they reveal one thing: individuals today are slaves to manuals, instruction booklets, handbooks, or prescriptions that spell out every move they are to make and that obviate the need for any real thinking or understanding on their part. Being so used to accepting the decisions of the experts, people are completely at sea when told that their own health and that of their children depend upon their level of judgment, their comprehension of the structure of the universe and its order.

It is traditionally assumed in the Orient that beyond the age of sixteen a young person will accept personal responsibility for his own state of being, be it happy or otherwise. Until that time, however, his parents are entirely responsible for him. He depends completely on their judgment.

Occidentals pay lip-service to this viewpoint by exclaiming, "What a wonderful idea — we are saved!" In actuality, they are frightened to death. And rightly so. For the average Westerner the acceptance of this viewpoint as his own involves a change of orientation that is profound enough to shake him to his very foundation since he therewith assumes full parental responsibility for his family. He can no longer, in good conscience, blame external circumstances for the difficulties his offspring encounter.

What, then is the solution? It appears to be as follows:

1. The serious individual should recognize that he is ignorant of the functioning of the universe, that modern life and its education have made him (and most men) a stranger to his natural instinct and intuition.

2. He should undertake an ever-deepening study of the philosophy of which macrobiotics is only a part.

3. He should establish a dynamic balance in his eating and

drinking, the prerequisite for growing comprehension and better judgment.

4. The student should use the principle of yin and yang in every phase of his life and in all things that he does, especially in the care of his young children.

What is needed is a faith in one's own judgment that can only come as a result of deep study (the true prayer and meditation). In such an atmosphere, fear and uncertainty vanish; there is no danger whatever — the path to health and happiness is open to both parents and children.

The great effectiveness of the macrobiotic method is rooted in the process of transmutation, without which nature as we know it (the human organism included) could not exist. Simply stated, it is the means whereby one element is changed into another, either naturally or artificially. This process, known and understood thousands of years ago by the sages of the Orient, enabled them to produce gold from other elements and to achieve combinations of metals and other substances that modern science can only duplicate with great difficulty, progress and mechanical devices notwithstanding.

I have always taught my students that they can transmute themselves from arrogant, diseased, materialistic men into humble, healthy, spiritual beings: that instead of being happy in appearance only and being killed by accident, murder or microbes or at the very least ending their lives as professional slaves, they can enjoy infinite freedom, eternal happiness and absolute justice for many long years. Now, after fifty years of effort on my part, there is proof that bio-chemical transmutation is neither the mystique of the alchemists of old nor just an abstract philosophical concept. It is a practical, living, verifiable reality.

On June 21, 1964 in Tokyo, I completed the transmutation

of the element sodium (Na) into potassium (K) under laboratory conditions of low temperature, pressure and energy. This significant achievement comes as a bombshell to science for until now, this type of reaction was thought possible only under conditions available in a high-energy particle accelerator. Our results were obtained, however, through the use of only a twenty-centimeter vacuum tube and a mere one hundred watts of power! (Further scientific evidence that substantiates the theory of bio-chemical transmutation is to be found in the revolutionary works of M. Louis Kervran, a French research biologist.[28] Our chance meeting in 1960 led directly to the startling event of June 21.)

The great significance of this discovery for parents is twofold:

1. It indicates that bio-chemical transmutation of elements is possible using the minute amounts of energy available in the human organism.

2. It is a verification of the foundation stone of macrobiotics, namely the understanding that through the process of transmutation, our bodies can produce all that they need for health from the simple diet that is a result of an understanding of the structure of the universe and its order.

Now, at last, what we have instinctively and intuitively known for thousands of years can be demonstrated in the laboratory. Man must not borrow elements from nature as he does when he doses himself with specifics such as iron, calcium, vitamin C, and sugar substitutes, to name only a few. He must be independent and manufacture his needs within his organism, by and for himself.

Claims that there is a need for externally-produced oil, protein, calcium, or vitamin C in the body can be answered as follows:

We have the capacity to manufacture what we need for health within our bodies. If we feed ourselves specific elements, this capacity withers from lack of use. Externally-produced elements must then be taken with regularity since the organism has given up the performance of its natural function. It has resigned in favor of artificial substitutes. We become slaves to the act of supplying our bodies with what we have been led to believe that they need.

We must, instead, be the creators from within of our own existence for we are the site of transmutation. Let us not turn that site into a morass through ignorance.[29]

A cow, for example, eats only grasses yet it has a very strong bone structure. Where does the calcium (Ca^{40}) that is required for these healthy bones come from?[30] Certainly not directly from the grass, a particularly poor source of that element. It is, however, a rich source of potassium (K^{39}). Hydrogen (H^1) is present in the cow's drinking water. The formula below outlines the natural, internal production of calcium in an organism through biological transmutation:

$$K^{39} + H^1 + \text{internal heat (activity)} \xrightarrow{\text{(forms)}} Ca^{40}$$

There is no reason to believe that the process in a human being would not be similar.

Human beings have digestive organs that can transmute chlorophyll into hemoglobin. In fact, all of what we eat is either transformed into blood (the prime source of raw material for our instant-by-instant re-creation of ourselves) or it is eliminated. For us, laboratory-produced calcium (inorganic because it is not the result of a living process) contaminates the blood and can be fatal.

In the process of bio-chemical transmutation, the most essential ingredient is activity, the by-products of which are oxygen and heat. (Activity keeps both the boa constrictor and the lizard alive under the high temperatures that are found in their natural habitats. If we immobilize either of these creatures, experimentally, it rapidly dies.) The natural tendency on the part of an average child to be tremendously active is very favorable to the maintenance of good health provided that his diet is simple and well-balanced in its yin and yang elements.

The parent faced by a special problem need have no fear. He has only two categories from which to choose — yin or yang. If changing the balance of the child's diet to the point where it is slightly more yin does not help, then the opposite (a balance slightly in favor of yang) will. Just bear in mind that each change in emphasis must be given time to take effect. Do not anxiously swing your child's diet back and forth. Try each for a reasonable length of time. Your thinking might go as follows: "What is the cause of my child's difficulty? It can only be too much yin or too much yang. I will try eliminating yin first. If after a reasonable time there is no change in the condition or if it gets worse, I will try the opposite way — the elimination of yang. The answer will show itself." The problem can thus be solved.

Let us consider the question of how much or how little salt to give a child. Movement will be our measuring stick. Too much salt or the total lack of it produces little activity. If a particular youngster is inactive and listless, if his natural tendency to move has been curtailed, salt should be decreased.

Where there is too much salt and little activity, there is no growth. With activity (the secret element in transmutation) at a minimum, the conversion of raw materials from a balanced diet into what the body requires, is upset. Elements other than calcium are produced, deficiencies result, and growth is arrested.

The process of transmutation goes on wherever there is life, no matter what sort of diet we follow. By understanding how it works, we can truly be the creators of ourselves and our existence. This is why our philosophy is called the philosophy of transmutation. Everything changes — illness becomes health, health become illness — into infinity.

The use of salt is an open question and varies from individual to individual. It graphically points up the need for us to think before acting. To illustrate: some people are in the habit of cooking with the same amount of salt for all persons in a family. If we consider no more than the difference in weight between an adult and a child, we can quickly see that the above method can lead to great difficulty. Let us say that an adult who weighs one hundred and fifty pounds uses one ounce of salt per week with good results. A fifteen-pound child that consumes the same amount of salt is in danger as indicated by the following table:

$$\text{Adult: } 150{:}1$$
$$\text{Child: } 15{:}1$$

For the proper ratio, the child should take only 1/10 of an ounce per week.

$$\text{Adult: } 150{:}1$$
$$\text{Child: } 15{:}1/10 = 150{:}1$$

Those who would follow the macrobiotic way should be keen observers who study and think in terms of yin and yang.

Whenever you cannot discover the cause of your child's suffering, give him only Diet No. 7 without adding salt, miso or soy sauce. If he has no appetite, prepare Diet No. 7 with much water (five to ten times more than usual) for a few days, a week, ten days or more.

Suppose a child is very quiet and has the tendency to lie down a great deal. We might jump to the conclusion that he is yin (silence and an exaggerated need to be horizontal are both symptoms of a yin condition) and treat him with yang. Further observation, however, reveals one other factor to be considered. The child expels little water, either by urination, sweating, running of the nose, or by way of tears. It is quite likely, therefore, that in spite of superficial yin symptoms, he is basically too yang. Treat him by using Diet No. 7, no salt, plus a very small quantity of apple or apple juice (yin).

We can safely draw the conclusion that a child until the age of six should have very little salt. For him, even a few grains can make all the difference.

Further, a child until the age of three has a good instinct about liquid. Let his desires guide you.

It is common knowledge that both fire and cold (frostbite) can cause burns of the skin. In each case the burn is produced by a different cause; consequently, each must be treated in a different manner. You must learn to see the large, over-all picture and not get lost in details. Think, think, and think some more.

Do not carry your child too much. Allow him the freedom to crawl, walk, and run — he needs this activity in order to maintain health. Do not allow your sentimental love to immobilize him.

Above all, learn from your children. Observe them carefully — they will teach you to have confidence in life rather than in medicine or the church. Each child has his own demand. Listen to it carefully and then give a little bit less.

The largest problem with children is their desire for large quantities of food and drink. The responsibility of the parents is to keep them slightly hungry and a bit on the cold side. Lower extremities should be uncovered when possible, bed covers should be light. This will help to produce a yang, hardy youngster. The parent whose judgment is on a sentimental level will find this very difficult to do for what is more of an accepted standard in our society than that our children should be warm and well fed at the very least? Nevertheless, try this method and you will be gratified by the results.

The maximum amount of vegetables for your child after his first birthday should be one-third of the total amount of grain in a meal. For example, three ounces of brown rice to one ounce of sauteed onions and carrots is adequate. Give very little oil. Each day, give the child a small amount of miso, soy sauce, and gomashio. (These all contain salt and should be considered when figuring the child's total intake of salt.)

No fish or meat is necessary at all. Neither is fruit. Examine the inside of your child's lower eye-lids periodically. They should be pink. If they are white, he is anemic — the composition of his blood is bad. You are feeding him foods that are too yin: too much vitamin C, fruit, sugar, etc.

If your child has a protruding stomach, his intestines are functioning poorly. You give him foods that are too expansive (yin). Establish a better over-all balance.

Bowel movements are also important. The color of the evacuation must be deep orange or light brown, agreeable to be seen and smelled. It should be long in shape, buoyant, and cohesive. The urine should be deep orange and transparent.[31]

The child who sucks his thumb is indicating that the chemical balance of his organism is off — he lacks iodine and calcium. The specific remedy for this is wakame, a Japanese sea-weed. Roast, crush, and sprinkle small amounts daily over his rice. Meanwhile examine your understanding of what constitutes the proper macrobiotic balance. For a reason that has to do with what you feed him, your child is not producing what he requires for health. Adjust his over-all intake of food so that he can manufacture his own iodine and calcium. A specific, symptomatic remedy like wakame will then no longer be necessary.

One potent source of anxiety for parents can be removed if one understands that according to Oriental philosophy, hereditary disease, as such, does not exist. If the opposite is true then the poor, sick, and the ignorant are condemned forever. The state in which they are born is irrevocably the state in which they remain unto death, doomed from the moment of conception. Then there is no transmutation of either the elements or more important, man. Yet we know that transmutation does occur. In addition, we know that nothing in this universe is constant. Everything is in a constant state of change. (The prime goal of the Occident is stability, security and constancy!) Heredity, therefore, is inconsequential. You can change your child from a dull, sickly individual into one who is supremely healthy and happy. All depends on your judgment, your comprehension and your application of yin and yang.

It is relatively easy to transmute the elements in the periodic table (the events of June 21 are witness to this). What is most difficult to do is to transmute arrogance into humility. For that, we must be 100 percent honest with at least ourselves. We must know this in order to be independent and free.

Remember, all babies are born happy — even the ones who enter into this life blind, deaf, or with some other deformity. They blissfully pulsate in the infinite where disabilities do not matter. It is the parents who are deeply and continually disturbed in the face of what they see as a handicap for their offspring in this relative, inconstant world. They superimpose their unhappiness on the children who are, as yet, oblivious. (The ability to judge relative qualities does not come until much later.) A lack of comprehension of the structure of the universe and its irrevocable order results in sadness for the ignorant parent, not for the child. This is true justice.

With concrete proof available that elements can be transmuted, that the phenomenon of biological transmutation actually exists in nature, the path is clear, at last, to the original goal of the philosophy of the Orient: the transmutation of man. What are the pitfalls to be avoided? There are none, for to become the healthiest man with the deepest comprehension of life, one must of necessity be the greatest adventurer.

In conclusion, I ask you to pose the following question to yourself: "What kind of an adult do I want my child to become — a doctor, a lawyer, a politician, a rich man, or the most happy, healthy, free human being?" Your answer will determine the direction that his education will take.

The education of the individual — the most important task that anyone can undertake — does not wait for the first day of pre-school nursery or kindergarten to begin. It starts in the home long before that for we influence our children from the very instant of conception.

Children are imitators. If their parents are interested only in material things like money and possessions, they will follow suit. They have no choice since during their formative years they are constantly in contact with the example that the parent sets.

If, however, you have educated yourself to understand that

the true goal for man is an infinite one — the attainment of eternal happiness, supreme health, absolute justice, complete freedom — then your child's future is assured. Life with a happy, healthy, just parent is the most complete education of all.

There are so many good reasons to be happy. We have air, water and light in abundance — all absolutely indispensable to the existence of life. They are a thousand times more precious than a diamond weighing two or three hundred carats! We have grasses, rivers, mountains, oceans and the sky. The heavens are full of galaxies that contain trillions of suns. They are ours! No one can take them away from us. So — merely by token of the fact that we exist, we are the happiest of beings. All living things are so happy — butterflies, birds, fish, microbes . . . they are dancing, amusing, making love . . . If we are unhappy, we are violating the order of the infinite universe.

If you are happy only occasionally, be careful. If your happiness is that which was given by others, was borrowed, bought or stolen (from parents, friends or schools) it is not yours and constitutes a debt. Such happiness will disappear sooner or later without exception. Happiness must be yours, completely — an independent achievement. It must be that which you yourself have created for yourself. Your health, your beauty, your judging ability, your knowledge must be yours.

First of all, you must be the creator of your health. All beings, grasses, trees, flies, microbes, animals, birds and even insects enjoy their own health, beauty, freedom and happiness. If yours have been given to you, you are the unhappiest person in the world. You are nothing but a liar! You are not you but others.

Three factors can assure success not only in dealing with yourself and your children, but also in all of living:

a. Study the philosophy of the Orient, applying its unique principle (yin-yang) on every level;

b. Practice macrobiotics;

c. Make many mistakes for they are our source of learning. Since everything changes, no error is irrevocable; there is nothing to fear.

We must transmute our lives, our health, our conception of all things, our thinking and our doing.

Macrobiotics and Old Age

Macrobiotically speaking, old age begins when an individual reaches his seventieth year. [According to Herman Aihara, Ohsawa said "eightieth year" in his lectures. -ed.]

For those who have lived from their youth through middle age and into their late years in accord with the order of the universe, there is no special diet; they are allowed to eat anything. Anything is used in the macrobiotic sense of the word: he who has lived in dynamic yin-yang balance for many years is so well-adjusted that he can control himself. His high level of judgment governs his choice of things to eat and drink so that he is able, figuratively to eat anything that he desires.

People who begin macrobiotics at or around the age of sixty had best follow my general directions for persons of all ages with the addition of the following advice:

1. Reduce salt intake; take very little as compared to a youth.

2. Eliminate oily or greasy foods (animal fats).

3. Use vegetable oil instead — a minimum amount.

You will be happy to know that many persons have cured

themselves late in life and have remained active beyond the age of eighty.

The essence of the macrobiotics of old age can be summed up in the phrase, "Live as close to nature as possible." In winter accept and know intimately the cold. In summer enjoy the heat. In springtime admire the flowers. In autumn compose poems about the moon. Live life with the feeling that you are harvesting the fruit of all your years. Give up all pettiness; be concerned with nature, with the vastness and unity of all existence.

The man of years spends his days in giving his personal happiness to others. In this sense, old age is the most joyful period of our lives. This kind of old age is the reward of those who have followed the order of nature.

If we want to end our lives happily, we had best prepare from an early age. We can thus be assured of that time of joy that consists in both the harvesting and the redistribution of happiness. Who could ask for anything more?

CHAPTER 12

On Cooking

1. Vegetables, cut or whole, should not be allowed to soak in water for a long time.

2. Do not peel any [naturally-grown] vegetable.

3. Eat as much rice and other cereals as you like but chew them well.

4. You may eat spoiled or decomposed cereals without fear. Your tired stomach will be grateful since it has no need to digest decomposed grain. Decomposition is digestion. Rice that is covered with mold is absorbed very easily.

5. Do not throw away even one grain of rice. If you do, you are a criminal and will be punished sooner or later. If everyone in the world were to throw away one grain per meal, we would lose 2,800,000,000 grains per meal or 2,800,000,000 x 3 x 365 grains annually. We could easily feed one million people for a year with this amount of food.

6. Eat those foods that do not protest or run away — vegetables, seaweeds, shell-fish.

7. Do not eat anything that is produced industrially or through a chemical process: these foods violate the law of the infinite universe.

8. You can eat anything that is in accord with the order of the infinite universe, e.g. fruit in season grown without chemical fertilizers or insecticides. This order is the absolute justice.

If the yearly production of apples in America is 180,000,000, you should eat only one apple per year. If you eat more than your share, you have stolen from your neighbors. Sooner or later, you will be punished by being sentenced to the prison called illness. What could be more just?

Salt — A New Superstition

Some thirty years ago, Professor Rene Quinton of the Sorbonne in Paris, published the theory that all biological beings on earth originally came from the sea. This concept, based on a life-long study of biology, is treated at length in his book. *L'Eau de Mer (Sea Water)*, and is accepted by scholars in science throughout the world.[32] The Quinton Institute in Paris and his laboratory-clinic on the Atlantic seashore are very famous, as is Quinton Plasma, which has been selling well for more than thirty years. His method "thalasotherapy" depends largely on the therapeutic use of salt.

The healthy functioning of the human body depends upon the establishment and maintenance of a good balance between sodium and potassium in the blood and the brain, yet the fear of salt dominates modern symptomatic medicine with no scientific basis at all for such an attitude.

Thanks to the discovery of fire and salt, both considered most precious since the beginning of recorded history, man has been able to create civilization as we know it. The importance of salt in ancient times is illustrated by the biblical term "salary" and the statement by Jesus that we are and must be the salt of the earth.

If your blood is deficient in salt, you surely suffer from acidosis. But why, you ask, is the fear of salt so prevalent today? This long story of the power of superstition is told in my book

Jack and Mitie in the West.[33]

Try a little salt, according to our macrobiotic cooking method for ten days. Try it for even one day. You will see that there is no danger involved at all. On the contrary, an improvement in your general health will result if you are guided by good judgment in its use. You will then begin to understand why there are so many so-called incurable diseases in the world today.

The number of clients in our macrobiotic restaurants in Paris, Brussels, Ghent and New York increases daily. These people have found that a few grains of salt can make a large difference in the state of their health.

Do not be frightened by a rumor born of superstition. Discover the truth by and for yourself — be independent!

Folk Medicine

America has its folk medicine and we in the Orient have ours, five thousand years old. Yours, unfortunately, has no philosophical, cosmological, or logical foundation; it is full of personal convictions that have not been filtered by the natural selection of thousands of years of experience. That this can be very dangerous is illustrated by the best-selling book *Folk Medicine.*[34] Its author indiscriminately recommends the mixture of honey and vinegar for everyone.

Myth and Vinegar

"Dr. Jarvis prescribes vinegar (always the cider variety) for all comers. The vinegar can be taken straight or diluted in the water. But for maximum efficacy, he insists that it be mixed with honey — a sort of sweet-'n'-sour, yang-and-yin combination." (*Time* magazine, Dec. 28, 1959.)

What a terrible mistake. First of all, honey and vinegar are both very yin. As a result, this mixture would be good for a few extremely yang persons and for a limited time. But, it might be fatal for those who suffer from yin diseases such as arthritis, asthma, cancer, high and low blood pressure, polio, rheumatism, or tuberculosis. I am certain that this method will be given up like many other new medicines, therapeutics, and dietetics. Until then, however, how many sick thousands will go from bad to worse, or even succumb to death?

Most of the dietary regimes that Americans are familiar with fail at a similar point. High-protein diets, low-calorie diets, low-sodium diets, fruit diets, liquid diets — the majority of them are the result of good intentions (plus the approval of the American Medical Association) but they are based upon neither long experience nor valid theory. They are empirical, non-scientific and what is most important, not founded on a solid principle of life. It is not surprising, therefore, that their effectiveness has usually been of the short-term variety. How many hundreds of individuals have turned to macrobiotics in desperation after having been subjected to this type of treatment?

By comparison, our list of macrobiotic foods and drinks has evolved naturally from the trial and error methods of millions of people over thousands of years, and was consolidated by our philosophy. As a further refinement, I have selected only those that are most correct and effective from both the theoretical and practical standpoints. The choice is not merely experimental or empirical: it is in accord with the philosophy of the structure of the infinite universe.

Your Case History

If you have established good health and have begun to contemplate new horizons of life, please send me a short history of your case. Educate your neighbors to the superiority of the macrobiotic way to health and happiness, particularly if they are suffering from the same disease as you. If you do not do this, you are not completely cured. You are still exclusive, antisocial, egoistic, and arrogant; you will surely fall ill again.

Exclusivity is both the most difficult disease in the world to cure and the origin of all unhappiness. One must be the sort of person who cannot possibly dislike any other human being. To love is to give and not to take in return. The give and take system is a mere egoism, for to give and give more is to become a creator. Since everything you have will sooner or later fade away, to give, give and give is to deposit in the unlimited bank, the Bank of Infinity. This is at the same time an infinite insurance policy that guarantees infinite life for you. The only premium that you pay is give, give and give. Give what? Give that which is the biggest and best gift in this world, health and eternal happiness, by means of the key to the kingdom of heaven. And, this key is simply the explanation of the structure of the infinite world and its unique principle translated into the language of macrobiotics, the art of longevity and rejuvenation. You can make yourself happy forever by distributing and establishing health and happiness, by discovering new horizons of joyful, amusing, and interesting living.

So, send me your experiences. They will encourage many other people. This is your first step in a new life, the true life of man.

Preview of the Death Certificate for a World Civilization

Fifth Report by an Old Oriental Philosopher

The twenty-fifth civilization is disappearing biologically, physiologically and psychologically. Why is this
modern Dinosaur becoming extinct?

Preface

The American World Empire (the Gold Dynasty), the monu-
mental achievement of modern civilization, is in the agonies
of its death. This finale seems to be the fatal destiny of human-
ity for it is occurring for the twenty-fifth time in the history of
the world. It derives from man's formally logical, analytical,
microscopic, mechanical, anatomical and scientific concept of
the universe. Further, the liquidation of the Western world
concept is taking place because of simple ignorance combined
with a lack of foresight: Americans have forgotten to study the
history of those civilizations that have preceded them. As
Alexis Carrel envisioned it some twenty-five years ago, the
closing scene of modern civilization is far more dramatic and
grandiose than that of the Roman Empire.[35]

At this crucial time, it is our duty to offer to the American
people the greatest gift that we have in the Orient — a supreme, invisible, ancestral treasure that is five thousand years
old. Since we have owed much to Western civilization from

the time of Admiral Perry's first visit to Japan one hundred years ago, our gift is offered as a partial payment of that debt. Humbly but with all confidence, we present the Unique Principle of freedom, health, happiness and world peace; it will be very useful and informative for our American friends.

(The great thinkers of the Orient have generally been ignored in the West as is illustrated by the attitudes of such eminent but exclusive thinkers as the coiners of American pragmatism — William James, John Dewey and Mortimer Adler, chief editor of the *Syntopicon.* Adler, in fact, was so exclusive that he originally baptized that work with the title *The Encyclopedia of Definitions of the World* although it contained little of the wisdom of the East. At the time, I was obliged to inform him that his "encyclopedia" was in actuality only half of one. Its title was subsequently changed to refer to the Western world only.)

The Unique Principle, yin-yang, was developed through our ancient philosophy. As compared to Western philosophy and science and technology which are deterministic, materialistic, analytical, anatomical and atomic, our viewpoint is paradoxical, dialectical, panoramic and universal — a system of all-embracing, unificative and creative contemplation. It is sometimes called "satori," "the Way of Zen," Mahayana Buddhism, Taoism, Shintoism or Vedanta.

The introduction into the Occident of this old theory of the Orient will be very interesting. Its biological and physiological technique — macrobiotics — is the application of that theory to the art of longevity and rejuvenation. It can change Western life completely. Here is the "Meeting of East and West" that can produce a distinguished new civilization.

1. Lectures in Los Angeles, San Francisco and New York:

Since my arrival in the United States last November, I have lectured on the philosophy and medicine of the Orient in Los Angeles, San Francisco and New York. I have faced enthusiastic audiences at the Universalist Church, the New School for Social Research, Columbia University, New York City College, the American Buddhist Academy and twice have had to postpone my departure for other lands. During this time, to my great happiness, I have confirmed my original assumption: a marriage between the paradoxical philosophy of the Orient and the materialistically precise techniques of American science can and must be consummated for the sake of world peace and the infinite freedom of Man.

Among those who attended my seminars were many who were miraculously cured of supposedly incurable diseases such as arthritis of twenty years' standing, prostatic cancer, high blood pressure, low blood pressure and mental illnesses. No medical or surgical treatment was used; the results were achieved only through biological and physiological means, the traditional macrobiotic directions fundamental to our philosophy.

In the United States there are 88,954,534 persons registered as victims of chronic disease.[36] Every American spends an average of $300 per year to fight disease and promote health.

$$\$300 \times 180,000,000 = \$54,000,000,000$$

This huge sum could very easily be saved if someone would mobilize American organizational and managerial techniques in order to industrialize, produce and distribute macrobiotic food products. These foods plus the Unique Principle offer health, freedom, happiness, independence and a sense of justice to every individual.

It would make me very happy if I could give the American people all the fruits of my sixty-seven years — the pragmatic, universal logic of Oriental philosophy and its biological, physiological application.

It is because of this philosophy and its medicine that Asiatic peoples lived for thousands of years in comparative happiness, disturbed only by local, limited war. The importation of Occidental civilization, however, with its total warfare, imperialism, and colonization, changed all that.

2. "Who's to start working up the 'God only knows' diagnosis?"

This is the despairing voice of American doctors in *Time* magazine, March 7, 1960.

According to Dr. W. Coda Martin, former Chief of the Geriatrics Clinic, Metropolitan Hospital, and Visiting Physician in Geriatrics for the Bird S. Coler Memorial Hospital, New York, "not only does half the population have some form of chronic disease, but only thirteen percent of the remainder are free of some type of physical defect." The following table reveals startling facts about the population of the United States:

Allergic disorders	20,000,000
Diseases of nervous system	15,000,000
Psychosis and psycho-neurosis	16,000,000
Arteriosclerosis and heart diseases	10,000,000
Mentally retarded children (one born every fifteen minutes)	3-5,000,000
Ulcers of stomach and duodenum	8,500,000
Cancer	700,000
Muscular dystrophy	100,000

Tuberculosis	400,000
(one hundred thousand new cases reported annually)	
Multiple sclerosis	250,000
Cerebral palsy	150,000
Defective vision	10,800,000
Various degrees of deafness	10,000,000
Sterility	15,000,000
Overweight	32,000,000
Alcoholism	4,000,000
Juvenile delinquency	2,000,000

Of some two hundred American soldiers who were killed in action and autopsied during the Korean conflict, approximately eighty percent were found to suffer from heart disease.

The incidence of heart disease among Americans has been compared to the Black Plague of the Middle Ages. Each year, two hundred thirty thousand men and one hundred thirty thousand women in this country die from heart attacks, and about one million more are incapacitated by less severe attacks.

Both Dr. Paul White, the physician who treated President Eisenhower following his heart attack, and Dr. Norman Joliffe, in charge of nutrition for the New York Department of Health, reported to Congress in 1956 that the United States is "one of the most unhealthy countries in the world" with regard to coronary heart disease. Dr. White has called heart disease "the modern American epidemic."

President Eisenhower told Congress, in 1954, that twenty-five million Americans living at that time would die of cancer unless the cancer mortality rate were lowered. (Perhaps ninety-five million more will succumb to heart disease unless something specific is done.)

Leukemia and lung cancer account for most of the current cancer deaths. Leukemia is the cause of approximately half of all the cancer deaths occurring in children under fifteen years of age, according to figures compiled by the Metropolitan Life Insurance Company.

Lung cancer, according to this company's statistics, accounts for nearly thirty percent of the total cancer mortality among men in the fifty-five to sixty-four range. ". . . This is at least 300 percent more than the comparable death rate from cancer of the stomach, the next leading site . . . " In Japan, by contrast, stomach cancer leads in the death rate marathon. Why? It is very simple. Lung cancer is more yin and stomach cancer is more yang if they are compared to one another. This means that the American killer, lung cancer, has subtle weapons — in the shape of the chemical, cybernetic food and drug industries — that are more effective and terrible than the ones available to its Japanese counterpart, stomach cancer. (Both the lungs and stomach are yin organs by virtue of the fact that they are empty organs. The lungs, however, because of their position in the body — a higher one as compared to the stomach — would be the more yin organ of the two. In addition, the function of the lungs is to deal with a gas, oxygen, which is yin while the stomach deals with solid matter, yang. Thus in order to be attacked by cancer, the stomach would require fewer yin factors than the lungs which would require more violent yin in greater quantity in order to be devastated.)

The large number of unexpected cancer cases among Americans has been disclosed by spot checks of apparently healthy people. In 1958, the routine examination of four hundred ninety-one supposedly well, active and employed men in New York City disclosed six cancers and thirty-six lesions that could lead to cancer, according to Dr. Walter E. O'Donnell of the Strang Cancer Prevention Clinic. Only one of the forty-two men with cancers and lesions had any symptoms that might cause him to go to a doctor.

During the same year, in another medical screening in New York City, two hundred ninety wives, all apparently well, were found to have a total of eighteen cancers. Twelve of the cancers were in the men, along with eighty-nine precancerous conditions and ninety-five benign tumors. The wives, in addition to having six cancers, had one hundred forty-seven precancerous conditions, one hundred nineteen of these conditions involving the breast and pelvic organs; the wives also showed eighty benign tumors. Wives and husbands, in addition, were found to have a total of three hundred sixty-two precancerous ailments.

More than 80 percent of these couples are preparing to disappear into the mouth of Man-eater No. 2 without knowing it. What a pity! This fact is more incredible than fiction if you consider it for a moment. If unknown to you, 60 or 80 percent of your body were on fire without your knowing why and without your knowing how to escape the approaching catastrophe, you would have no need to fear going to Hell. You would be there already, complacently surrounded by comfort, medicine, insurance, and most of all sickness.

The picture of the nation's mental health is even darker. One American out of ten spends part of his life in a mental hospital. "And it's getting worse. We are in more trouble than we thought," said M. Gorman, executive director of the National Committee on Mental Health. According to scientist Alexis Carrel the problem was out of hand some twenty years ago.[37] Yet up until the present time the medical profession is still protected by law and government, notwithstanding its startling ignorance of health, life and happiness, and its apparent inability to prevent disease.

Throughout the nation, people suffer from still other serious chronic ailments. In the winter months of 1957 alone, according to the National Institute of Health, more than one hundred million Americans suffered from respiratory illnesses. It is interesting to note that no wild animal suffers from similar complaints in cold weather. To my knowledge not a single deer, sparrow or fish in the forests or icy rivers suffered from a cough or cold throughout the entire New York winter of 1959-60. On the contrary, they all enjoyed the weather without heat or costly overcoats. The more that food and warmth grew scarce, the more beautiful they became.

Civilized man has lost this dynamic adaptability, his key to infinite freedom. He has unknowingly replaced it with the finite and conditional liberty that is also known as sensory satisfaction. This liberty of slaves or prisoners is enticingly but mistakenly called comfort, pleasure, or high standard of living. Herein lies the largest defect in modern democracy. It is the crime of mechanical civilization.

3. How much does one spend to kill a civilization?

Medication costs the United States a total of $54,000,000,000 per year. This is a very big loss. In addition to the amount paid for formal medical care, fortunes are spent for various remedies that are consumed by the ton to relieve insomnia, discomfort, and pain:

Aspirin	some 15,000,000 lbs.
Sleep-inducing drugs	more than $100,000,000

Further losses can be estimated as follows:

Illness absence	$5,000,000,000
Prolonged illness absence	1,777,000,000
Government expenses for health	2,500,000,000

Add to this the huge sum being spent for cancer research. And
the unbelievable amounts expended for the manufacture of
atomic and hydrogen bombs specifically designed to annihi-
late civilization. Plus the cost of industrialized, chemical, can-
cer-producing food and drink! Such is the price of the destruction of the American World Empire. All this because the
American ability to judge on a high level has been eclipsed
through total ignorance of the order of the infinite universe
and its unique justice.

The responsibility for this great threat to America rests
upon its leaders in religion, education and medicine.

4. The real cause of disease, unhappiness and war.

First, there is only one cause for all disease according to
the philosophy of the Orient: ignorance of the structure of the
universe and its unique principle. Through our study of this
philosophy, however, we can eliminate our ignorance. We can
go on to cure disease by and for ourselves without medication
or operations merely by eating strictly in accordance with the
existing natural order.

Secondly, violation of this order in daily behavior is the
basic cause for the unhappiness of man. Since behavior is governed by judgment which is easily clouded by poor eating and
drinking, unhappiness can only be cured by a new biological
education in accordance with the order of the universe.

Lastly, four factors are prerequisite to a state of war:

1. Two or more governments that are ignorant of the order
of the infinite universe.

2. People who are also ignorant of that order.

3. Crystallized fear in the shape of machines for killing.

4. A faith or confidence in violence that is characteristic of
those who know nothing of the structure of the infinite uni-

verse.

These four factors are essentially variations on the same basic theme — lack of comprehension.

The philosophy of health and happiness tells us that a way of living that is peaceful, joyful and provocative of deep thought can be achieved by following strictly the order of the infinite universe in our diet. The natural consequence of such an existence is a happy and healthy home that is also in accord with that same order. Orderliness in our lives in relation to all things is possible with this unique principle as our guide.

If everyone were to observe this unique, dialectical and paradoxical law on every level of life, world peace would be realized spontaneously. No costly social reform or bloody, destructive revolution would ever be necessary.

5. Professional education and invalid religion.

During these four winter months, I have yet to see a child or young student in the subway, on the street, or at the universities who could score even sixty out of the one hundred points possible in the Seven Main Conditions of Health and Happiness that I have been teaching for forty years. From the standpoint of his judgment, the average American scores a zero. He is no longer accustomed to thinking; he has become the victim of a "let-someone-else-do-it," push-button existence. Americans, educated in a manner that is too pragmatic and encyclopedic, are taught to be good professionals — machine-men or slaves. They do not think. In 1644, Pascal said, "Man is a thinking reed" and went on to invent the calculating machine. In the America of today, he would surely say, "Man is a non-thinking cow." The cow, you remember, is born to be exploited and never knows the freedom that wild animals take for granted throughout their lives.

In the United States, more than in any other country, I have been shocked by the number of people who cannot use their innate ability to judge. They have eyes and ears but they do not see or hear. They are only suspicious! They know the relative, limited and ephemeral world where nothing is constant; where happiness, freedom and justice are short-lived. They neither know nor want to know the absolute and eternal Mother of all — the infinite world. The very sound and sight of the word infinity repels them.

Temples and churches are visited more frequently in this materialistic, scientific land than in the very religious country of India. This contradiction should provoke much thought. Is it not strange that inveterate church-goers are the very people who do not want to know infinity, the very ones who are so attached to the relative, material world?

Their religion and ethics, like all others, preaches:

> Love thine enemy . . .
> Give up everything — even life — and follow me.
> Turn the other cheek . . .

Yet I have not met one person here who observes these fundamental teachings. For example, law — the crystallization of violence — severely attacks the enemies of society rather than loving them. It even condones the death penalty for certain crimes. Why does no one turn the other cheek? The real criminals, the educators, are rarely brought to justice. Would it not make more sense to punish those who create gangsters and delinquents rather than the delinquents and gangsters themselves?

To go further, organized medicine attacks microbes, viruses and other imaginary enemies of man. Yet all of these organisms are creations of God, just as men are. Medicine does not love them. It neither asks why God created them in the first place and re-creates them day in and day out, nor why and how some men are attacked by them while others are not. It appears that Oriental medicine alone finds their existence in the healthy human a natural state of affairs.

In addition, the war industry operates in the name of justice, peace and freedom. Can justice be destructive? Can peace be bloody? Can freedom be won by violence?

Bertrand Russell has said that we are living in a world of insanity.[38] Is civilization psychotic? Are not the lack of supreme judging ability and insanity one and the same thing?

In the eyes of this old Oriental philosopher, all the unhappiness and misery of the twentieth-century World Gold Empire are caused by the invalid religion and professional education that perpetuate blind eating and drinking.

As a result of my open criticism, you might take me to be an enemy of this World Empire. You would be quite wrong, however, for I am in truth its admirer. My all-embracing philosophy can and does include even an Empire such as this one. It discards nothing; it is the unifying and mediating principle. Its prime reason for being is to show that all antagonisms are complementary.[39] Western civilization, therefore, has nothing to give up. It can continue its usual activity. It has only to be guided by clearer judgment which will point out a new direction. My recommendation of the philosophy of the Orient with its paradoxical dialectics is purely for the purpose of justifying and fortifying the Western way of life.

6. The last despairing cry of organized medicine.

Every kingdom divided against itself is brought to desolation; and every city or house divided against itself shall not stand.   —Matthew 12:25

In *Time* magazine for March 7, 1960, there is a very important article called "The Limited Specialist" that confirms my observations and conclusions with reference to the health and medicine of America.

The more that analytical, microscopic medicine advances, the more it demands specialization. (Medicine without specialists is a peacock without feathers while analytical science without analytical techniques is nothing; its motivating force is gone.) There are now so many medical specialties that patients cannot find their way through this maze that grows in complexity every day. Segmentation has gone so far that the specialists themselves are confused.

Frustration was apparent after one thousand eighty-one physicians of all types were polled by *Medical Economics*.[40] No fewer than ninety-one percent were worried about jurisdictional disputes and were admittedly uncertain over the problem of where to draw the line:

> Though most specialists agree that something should be done for their own peace of mind and also the patients' benefit, they have few constructive suggestions. More characteristic is the despairing plaint: "Who's to start working up the 'God only knows' diagnosis?" To that, neither confused specialists nor confused patients had an answer.

These complaining specialists, the most advanced men in analytical medical science, surely symbolize the despair of Occidental medicine. Their desperation is an honest confession of the fact that analytical medicine has reached a dead end. It is the death knell of a medicine that has damaged (and in some instances killed) the very people who created the civilization out of which it was born. Since the last words of a dying man are usually truthful, "God only knows" is entirely appropriate. No one among confused patients and discouraged medical specialists has the answer.

Miraculously, however, there are right now some hundreds of Americans who can declare with all confidence, "I know the divine medicine." They have found true health to be the sum of justice, freedom and happiness — a totality that is universal, creative, contemplative and infinitely adaptable. At my lectures and seminars they have seen many wonderful restorations of life — the cure of physical and mental disease by correct natural eating and drinking without costly up-to-the-minute medicines or treatments.

The divine medicine that I have been interpreting for forty-seven years is the Unique Principle applied to daily life. It, in turn, is the core of the five-thousand-year-old philosophy of yin and yang, the biological and physiological foundation of all the religions of the Orient.[41] My method is not one that destroys symptoms by violence; it is a philosophy of happiness and justice, so simple and practical that anyone can practice it immediately under all circumstances.

From our viewpoint, the only one able to cure a sufferer is the sufferer himself, for a man must be independent first of all. Health, the synthesis (coming together) of freedom, justice, peace and happiness, cannot and must not be given by others. Even if it could be given, it would only create a life-long debt. Yet this treasure — health — was given billions of years ago and has been free for the taking ever since to all who can see, hear and think. The wild animals who live so happily bear witness to that fact.

7. The Physiological and Medical Revolution in Mao-tse-tung's China:

According to an article in the *New York Times Magazine* (Feb. 28, 1960) entitled "Medicine in China: A Revolution Story," the China of Mao-tse-tung has begun a new physiological and medical revolution — the first, and probably the last, in history.

The writer, Miss Peggy Durdin, quite obviously a stranger to medicine, biology, psychology, philosophy and perhaps the Chinese language as well, has made many mistakes in her report. (This is traditional with Occidental journalists in the Orient.) Nevertheless, there is one extremely important fact in her article: seventy thousand Chinese doctors who practice Western medicine have been ordered to learn the traditional Chinese medicine that is still used by half a million healers.

It is not widely known that when Western medicine was imported into the Orient during the last century, all traditional practitioners were gladly granted official government permission to use the new method. This act of tolerance has no parallel in Western history and contrasts sharply with the fact that Western peoples have imported only one thing from the East, namely Christianity (some eighteen centuries ago). They have since shut their doors to all things philosophical that originate in the Orient while taking everything that could afford them pleasure and comfort: gold, silver, diamonds, petroleum, precious stones, spices, perfumes, indigo. Thus England and France were able to build up powerful empires while blandly violating their Christian faith.

Oriental people have given of all their wealth and even their ancestral lands. They have truly followed the teaching of Jesus: "Resist ye no evil; but whosoever shall smite thee on thy right cheek, turn to him the other side." If today these same people are in revolt against the recent invader from the West, they are either being faithful to the invader's teaching or are tired of his Christian hypocrisy. For them, Westernized Christianity is their unique and beloved daughter who has been kidnapped, violated, mutilated, and then abandoned.

Apparently, feelings in the Orient are just as strong with regard to medicine.

Everything changes in this relative and rotating world, monopoly and authority included. Nothing is final or static. Everything that has a front also has a back — a good side and a bad side. All that begins, must end. The bigger the front, the bigger the back. Where there is utility, there is inutility; where there is advantage, there is disadvantage. Only these principles of universal logic are valid. There is nothing in the universe but yin and yang (front and back, beginning and end).

The medicine of today is much too monopolistic, a virtual dictatorship without tolerance of self-criticism. Yet, one of the founding fathers of this country pleaded for tolerance in medicine.[42] I pay homage to him. May I hope that his visionary understanding will become recognized once more?

8. The "God only knows" medicine (the biological and physiological foundation of all great religions in the Orient):

If Mortimer Adler had compiled a complete *Syntopicon* that had included both Occidental and Oriental wisdom, American doctors might easily find the "God only knows" medicine and end their despair. Through outright neglect of the fact that all the great thinkers of the Orient were primarily teachers who understood and pointed the way to health by way of happiness, Adler and his collaborators revealed that their own concept of life and the universe was far from being either practical or complete.

Without knowing how to establish absolute health, one cannot teach the way to happiness. For that reason, all the great religions and philosophies of the Orient based their medicine on the structure of the infinite universe. Unfortunately, the leaders and scholars of the Western world are strangers to the Oriental mind and philosophy. Their understanding is blocked by both their personal mental Daltonism and the lack of adequate interpreters.[43] For example, Levy-Bruhl, the late president of the French Philosophical Society, called the Oriental mentality (including its philosophy and its concept of the infinite universe) a "Mentalite Primitif" in all four of his life-works.[44] Dr. Albert Schweitzer has shown a similarly limited understanding.[45] Both because of and in spite of this, I cannot remain indifferent to the official, despairing voice of American doctors.

I have lived for sixty-seven years in the philosophical climate of the Orient where my life was saved only because Western doctors decided I was beyond help. I thus had the good fortune to avoid the tragic fate of the rest of my family, all of whom had put their trust in Western medicine: my mother died at the age of thirty, two sisters died before they were ten, and my one younger brother succumbed at sixteen. I alone was saved by the ancient medicine of the Orient. After this narrow escape at eighteen, I decided to dedicate the rest of my life to the task of telling people about that old and supposedly obsolete medicine, a goal that I have achieved. (A few days after my sixtieth birthday, I left Japan forever, successively spending two years in India, one year in the jungles of darkest Africa — most in Dr. Schweitzer's hospital — and five years in European countries.) I have constantly taught the way to establish health and happiness through eating and drinking according to Oriental philosophy.

As a result I have made thousands of friends in European countries, some of whom have opened macrobiotic restaurants and clinics. Health food shops everywhere deal in natural foods that are in accord with macrobiotic principles. Factories and farms in France, Japan and the United States produce macrobiotic food and drink:

> Ohsawa coffee made from cereals
> Grain milk (kokkoh) in powder form
> Ohsawa bread
> Whole brown rice
> Poti-marron (my name for the Japanese pumpkin
>   that can cure any diabetic in ten days)
> Azuki beans (small red beans that are good for kid-
>   ney disease)
> Lotus root (a root that cures the most desperate case
>   of asthma in a week or two)
> Ohsawa tamari (natural soy sauce produced by the
>   traditional, biological, sugarless method)

During one of my seminars, I made the following statement to my students: "Now that you have studied Oriental philosophy and its biological, physiological application called macrobiotics, you can see that this practical method is capable of leading you towards absolute health and infinite happiness. In a short time you have found yourselves able to contemplate horizons of life that are completely new. You must answer the despairing cry of doctors by shouting: 'Here is the divine philosophy that can be applied biologically and physiologically to everyday life. With it, we can at last establish absolute health and happiness!'

"By doing this, you can save your country billions of dollars each year. You can be businessmen on this high financial level by utilizing that American specialty — organizational and managerial know-how — to teach macrobiotics and the way to establish health and happiness through eating and drinking. It could become the first biological and physiological revolution in the history of man."

Everyone applauded.

I sincerely hope the enthusiasm of my students will not stop there. I trust that they will not become exclusive and self-satisfied — contentedly enjoying their own personal cures while others are still suffering in ignorance. I am confident that they will do their best to teach macrobiotics and the philosophy it is based upon (once also the foundation of what both Jesus and Moses taught their neighbors).

Since I have spent all my life in the simple role of an interpreter of Oriental philosophy, you can well imagine how happy I would be if I could bring together the Far West and the Far East. Their union alone can create world peace and infinite freedom for Man forever.

The Western world imported Christianity from the Orient long ago, not without difficulties. Since then, Christianity has become symbolic, obsolete and impractical as a solution for daily individual and social problems. We must begin to use a new, biological, physiological and practical interpretation of the Christian everyday guide to absolute health and infinite happiness. Herein lies the true significance of the "Meeting of East and West."

9. My New Prophecy:

Ten months before Pearl Harbor, I published three books:

Standing on the Front Line of the Health War

The Last and Eternal Winner
Who Are Those Who Destroy Japan?

In these books, I prophesied:

1. The desperately tragic death of Gandhi,
2. the end of British colonization in India,
3. the complete defeat of Japan for the first time in 2,600 years,
4. the fall of the Gold Dynasty, the American World Empire.

The first and second predictions were an actuality five years later; the third, six years later; the fourth, seventeen years later, in the form of pandemic mental and physical disease.

During the past forty-seven years, I have made many prophecies relating to individual, social, national and international questions, almost all of which have been realized. This ability to prophesy is not some variety of mystical, metaphysical or occult divination, but simply biological and physiological foresight.

After four winter months in the United States, I am making a new prophecy:

> Were American understanding of the Oriental mentality and philosophy to be deepened, and were Mortimer Adler (compiler of the *Syntopicon*) to compile another semi-encyclopedia that encompasses the Oriental world, there would no longer be any source for future wars; a new civilization could continue for at least two thousand years.

I therefore advise you to organize a small group for research into Oriental philosophy. An understanding of the structure and the order of the infinite universe will give you faith. With faith, nothing will be impossible for you. You can even say to the mountain, "Remove hence to yonder place."

You are the salt of the earth. You can change your destiny! You can give birth to a new civilization or you can create Hell on earth.

Conclusion

Coming to the United States, I have seen the symptoms of the fall of the twenty-fifth civilization. I have found some enthusiastic friends with whom I have shared my knowledge of Oriental philosophy and its medical translation, macrobiotics.

The winter months have passed and spring shows signs of happiness. This is order in the relative and defined world. Yang follows yin and vice versa. The bigger the difficulty, the bigger the happiness.

My dear new friends in America, how happy we are! You and I, so little and so limited in this relative world, have been able to meet and understand each other because we have been good friends in the world of Infinity . . . long, long ago . . . long, long ago.

Meeting is the beginning of separation. I am departing but I will come again at any time should you need me.

Spring returns every year . . .

The Order of the Universe

1. That which has a face has a back. (Negation of the law of identity and contradiction in space.)

2. That which has a beginning has an end. (Negation of the above in time.)

3. There is nothing identical in the universe. (Negation of the law of identity.)

4. The bigger the face, the bigger the back. (Negation of the law of the exclusive middle.)

5. All antagonisms are complementary, for example, beginning-end, front-back, justice-injustice, freedom-slavery, happiness-unhappiness, rise-fall, expansion-contraction, love-hate. (Negation of formal logic.)

6. All antagonisms can be classified in two categories — yin and yang — and they are complementary. (Foundation of universal dialectic logic.)

7. Yin and yang are the two arms of Infinity, Absolute Oneness, God, or the Infinite pure expansion.

Twelve Theorems of the Unique Principle

1. Yin and yang are the two poles of the infinite pure expansion.

2. Yin and yang are produced infinitely, continuously, and forever from the infinite pure expansion itself.

3. Yin is centrifugal; yang is centripetal. Yin, centrifugal, produces expansion, lightness, cold, etc. Yang, centripetal, produces constriction, weight, heat, light, etc.

4. Yin attracts yang; yang attracts yin.

5. All things and phenomena are composed of yin and yang in different proportions.

6. All things and phenomena are constantly changing their yin and yang components. Everything is restless.

7. There is nothing completely yin or completely yang. All is relative.

8. There is nothing neuter. There is always yin or yang in excess.

9. Affinity or force of attraction between things is proportional to the difference of yin and yang in them.

10. Yin expels yin; yang expels yang. Expulsion or attraction between two things yin or yang is in inverse proportion to the difference of their yin or yang force.

11. Yin produces yang; yang produces yin in the extremity.

12. Everything is yang at its center and yin at its periphery (surface).

The Seven Stages of Judgment[46]

VII. **Supreme:**
Absolute and universal love that embraces everything and turns every antagonism into complementarity.

VI. **Ideological:**
Based upon thinking power and thought — justice and injustice.

V. **Social:**
Motivated by social reason: morals and economy.

IV. **Intellectual:**
Conceptual, scientific.

III. **Sentimental:**
Desirable and undesirable.

II. **Sensory:**
Pleasant and unpleasant.

I. **Physical:**
Mechanical and blind judgment.

The Seven Stages of Illness[47]

I. **Fatigue:**
Caused by an orderless life (undisciplined, mean, ungrateful) or a chaotic family or parents.

11. **Pain and Suffering:**
Caused by low judgment (capricious, sensorial, sentimental, conceptual, exclusive) and psychomatic illness.

III. **Chronic Symptoms:**
Leading to headache, painful chest, diarrhea, vomiting, ulcer, trachoma, leukemia, all skin and blood diseases: Caused by an excess of yin or yang in foods, resulting from the love or hate of certain foods.

IV. **Sympathicotonia or Vagotomy:**
Illness has ascended to the autonomic nervous system.

V. **Functional and Structural Changes**
of the organs themselves.

VI. **Psychological or Emotional Disease:**
Schizophrenia, neurasthenia, hysteria, cardiac dilation, etc.

VII. **Spiritual Disease:**
This afflicts those of such good physical constitution that they by-pass the first six stages. They suffer unconsciously from their arrogance and intolerance. Despite outer success, they are without faith, hope, joy and love and they always end tragically.

Classification of the Origin of Man's Thoughts and Actions[48]

Stage of Judgment	Learning	Love	Profession	Eating and Drinking
7th SUPREME	Self-realization, illumination, Tao, satori	All-embracing	Happy man, fulfills all his dreams throughout life	Eat and drink anything with great pleasure
6th IDEOLOGICAL	Philosophy, religion, dialectics	Spiritual	Thinker, originator of theories	Follow a dietetic or religious principle
5th SOCIAL	Economics, morality	Social	Organizer	Conformist—"like everyone else"
4th INTELLECTUAL	Science, arts	Understanding, scientific, systematic calculating, expert	Wholesaler of knowledge and techniques	According to a theory of nutrition
3rd SENTIMENTAL	Literature	Emotionally universal	Wholesaler of emotions	Gourmet (connoisseur)
2nd SENSORY	Dance, gymnastics, techniques, conditioned reflexes	Erotic, physical comfort-seeking, sensual pleasure	Wholesaler of pleasure: merchant, novelist, actor, prostitute	Gourmand (greedy eater)
1st MECHANICAL, BLIND	Instinctive or unconscious reflexes	Instinctual (appetite, hunger)	He who sells his life—working slave, salaried employee	Guided only by hunger and thirst
	Unimaginative teachers, concerned with data alone, are at the 1st stage			

Dictionary of Macrobiotic Terms

Azuki	Japanese red bean
Ae	Dressing (vegetables) with soybean paste, orange juice, etc.
Aemono	Japanese salad
Agé	Fried bean curd
Akaza	Wild spinach
An	Red bean jam
Ankake	Pouring jam
Aoza	Wild spinach
Azami	Thistle
Bancha	Coarse green tea roasted a few minutes
Bansho	Bancha with natural soy sauce
Chana	Indian grain
Chapati	Baked or fried round pancakes (Indian cooking)
Chirashi Zushi	Rice preparation
Daikon	Long, white Japanese radish
Dango	Dumpling
Dentie	Head of eggplant — salted, stored, dried, burned and ground into a powder.
Egoma	Variety of sesame seed — most yang.
Gobo	Burdock
Gomashio	Sesame salt
Goma Tofu	Sesame curds
Gomoku	Mixing (boiled riced, noodles or beans) with vegetables
Goziru	Soup made of grated soy beans and vegetables (*Ziru* means soup in Japanese)
Gyoza	Vegetable mixture wrapped in thin dough (Chinese)

Hako	A mold or box
Hiba, Hoshina	Dried leaves of Japanese radish
Hiziki	Spindle-shaped, small, black seaweed
Huki	Coltsfoot
Jinenjo	Wild potato or Japanese yam
Kake	Pouring (cooked vegetables or boiled water over noodles)
Kaki	Stirring with water (buckwheat flour)
Kampyo	Dried gourd strips
Karinto	Deep-fried cookie
Kasha	Russian buckwheat grain preparation
Kayu	Thin porridge or rice preparation
Kinpira	Mixture of burdock and carrots
Kinton	Pastry made of boiled chestnuts and apples
Kitune	Boiled rice or noodles cooked with thin fried bean curds
Kobu, Kombu	Sea vegetable found in deep ocean waters
Kobu Maki	Kobu (kombu) stuffed with vegetables
Kohren Tea	Dried and powdered lotus root boiled in water
Koi-Koku	Special carp-and-miso soup
Kokkoh	Creamed blended cereal
Konnyaku	Paste made from flour of Japanese tuberose
Kuri	Chestnut
Kuwai	Arrowhead
Kuzu	Powdered plant "gelatin" obtained from kuzu root
Mu Tea	Tea made from blended herb roots
Matuba	Pine leaves
Miso	Soybean paste
Miso Ae	Boiled vegetables served with miso cream
Misoni	Carrots and onions cooked with miso
Mochigome	Glutinous rice

Mori	Heaping on a bamboo basket (wheat or buck-wheat vermicelli)
Moti	Rice cake
Muso	Spread prepared from sesame butter and miso
Musubi	Knot
Nazuna	Shepherd's purse
Nishime	Slowly cooked vegetables
Nitsuke	Sautéed vegetables
Nobiru	Wild scallion
Nori	Laver or sloke (variety of seaweed)
Ogura	Azuki (red bean) preparaton
Omedeto	Roasted rice and red bean dessert. Originally, Japanese word for congratulations
Ositasi	Boiled vegetables served with soy sauce
Ransho	Egg and soy sauce preparation
Renkon	Lotus root
Sakura	Cherry blossoms or their color — pink
Sarashina	Variety of buckwheat dish. Originally, the name of place famous for good buckwheat
Sato-imo	Japanese name for albi, yutia or taro plant (tube-rose)
Shahan	Rice-vegetable preparation (Chinese)
Shiitake	Variety of Japanese mushroom
Shio	Salt
Shio Kombu	Seaweed preparation
Soba	Buckwheat noodle
Sukiyaki	Fish or beef and vegetables cooked together
Sushi	Rice preparation
Sho-ban	Coarse green tea and soy sauce
Tahini	Sesame butter
Tai	Red snapper (fish)
Tamari	Liquid left after making miso in the traditional

	way [previously used to mean traditional (natural) soy sauce made without chemicals -ed.]
Tekka	Mixture of minced lotus root, burdock root, carrot, ginger and miso
Tempura	Japanese process of deep-frying in oil
Tofu	White soybean cheese
Tororo	Wild potato; also, the inner part of kombu, finely grated
Udon	Wheat vermicelli, noodle or macaroni
Umeboshi	Japanese plum salted and preserved for 3 years
Ume-sho-ban	Medicinal beverage
Yaki	Toasting, baking, roasting, frying
Yanagawa	Loach — freshwater fish related to carp
Yannoh	Ohsawa cereal coffee
Yomogi	Mugwort or wormwood
Yuba	Soybean protein in transparent, papery sheets
Zaru	Bamboo basket
Zosui	Rice preparation

Footnotes

Foreward
1. See the writings of Lao-tse, Buddha and Sun Tzu-wu.

Preface
2. The word **Macrobiotic** is derived from the Greek:
   macro — great, comprehensive, unobstructed
   bio — life
   biotic — way of life, technique of rejuvenation

Chapter 1
3. *The Manual of Epictetus* (Oxford, 1916).

4. George Ohsawa, *The Philosophy of Oriental Medicine* (George Ohsawa Macrobiotic Foundation, Oroville, California, 1991). Previously titled, *The Book of Judgment.*

5. A. J. Toynbee, *A Study of History* (London, 1935), Vol. I, page 201.

6. For Yin-Yang theory see page 110 of this volume.

Chapter 2
7. Whereas the word **disease** implies a deterioration of vital functions (health → disease), the word **cure** implies the halting of this deterioration, a reversal of direction (disease → health). A cure has been achieved when one recognizes the Order of the Universe in all things. Modern medicine, by contrast, is content to call the dissipation of symptoms a cure.

8. A. J. Toynbee, *A Study of History* (London, 1935) Vol. IV, page 6.

9. Live the life of unfettered simplicity.

Chapter 3
10. Cybernetic pertains to the comparative study of automatic control systems formed on the one hand by the human nervous system and brain, and on the other by electrical-mechanical communications systems.

11. Dr. S. Margine, *Medical Essay and Observation* (Edinburgh, 1747).

12. Address, delivered at Boston (June, 1930).

13. For Yin-Yang theory see page 110 of this volume.

14. A. J. Toynbee, *A Study of History* (London, 1935) Vol. I, page 205.

Chapter 4
15. See Buddhism, Christianity, Hinduism, Islam, Jainism, Judaism, Shintoism, Taoism.

16. George Ohsawa, *The Philosophy of Oriental Medicine* (George Ohsawa Macrobiotic Foundation, Oroville, California, 1991). Previously titled, *The Book of Judgment*.

Chapter 5
17. See page 117 of this volume.

18. For detailed information, see William Longgood. *The Poisons in Your Food* (New York, 1960).

19. For specific recipes see *The First Macrobiotic Cookbook* (George Ohsawa Macrobiotic Foundation, Oroville, California, 1986).

Chapter 8
20. Blaise Pascal, "Pensees," *Great Books* (Encyclopedia Britannica) Vol. XXXIII, section vi, page 347.

21. F.S.C. Northrop, *The Meeting of East and West* (New York, 1947), page 316 ff.

22. George Ohsawa, *The Philospohy of Oriental Medicine* (George Ohsawa Macrobiotic Foundation, Oroville, California, 1991), page 60.

Chapter 9
23. Eugen Herrigel, *Zen in the Art of Archery* (New York, 1953).

24. Must be fed organic, whole grains.

25. Must be fertilized. See page 117 of this volume.

Chapter 10

26. Available from the Centre Ignoramus, Paris [in the 1960s].

27. If your wife or husband does not fit this description, do not worry. Macrobiotic living can transmute your mate into someone who is ideal for you.

Chapter 11

28. C. Louis Kervran, *Transmutation Biologiques* (Paris, 1962). *Transmutations Naturelles* (Paris, 1963).

29. From a lecture by George Ohsawa at the Second Annual Macrobiotic Summer Camp, Plaskett Creek, California, August 4, 1964.

30. Superscript numbers, e.g. Ca^{40}, indicate the atomic weight of an element.

31. George Ohsawa, *The Philosophy of Oriental Medicine* (George Ohsawa Macrobiotic Foundation, Oroville, California, 1991), page 33.

Chapter 12

32. Rene Quinton, *L'Eau de Mer* (Paris, 1912).

33. Available through the George Ohsawa Macrobiotic Foundation in study edition only.

34. D.C. Jarvis, M.D., *Folk Medicine* (New York, 1959).

Appendix 1

35. Alexis Carrel, *Man, the Unknown* (New York, 1939), page xiii.

36. William Longgood, *The Poisons in Your Food* (New York, 1960). All statistics in Appendix II are taken from this volume.

37. Alexis Carrel, *Man, the Unknown* (New York, 1939), p. 112 ff, p. 154 ff.

38. *New York Times*, April 4, 1961, p. 22.

39. See page 32, fifth paragraph.

40. *Medical Economics* (Oradell, N.J.).

41. Buddhism, Christianity, Islam, Judaism, Shintoism, Taoism.

42. L. H. Butterfield, *Letters of Benjamin Rush* (Princeton, N.J., 1951), Vol. II, page 249.

43. Daltonism: Materialism as opposed to spirituality.

44. L. Levy-Bruhl, *The "Soul" of the Primitive* (New York, 1928), page 318.

45. Albert Schweitzer, *Les Grands Penseurs de l'Inde* (Paris, 1952). page 131 ff.

Appendix II

46. George Ohsawa, *The Philosophy of Oriental Medicine* (George Ohsawa Macrobiotic Foundation, Oroville, California, 1991), page 143.

47. George Ohsawa, *The Philosophy of Oriental Medicine* (George Ohsawa Macrobiotic Foundation, Oroville, California, 1991), page 122.

Bibliography

Butterfield, H. H., *Letters of Benjamin Rush*, Princeton: Princeton, 1951.

Carrel, Alexis, *Man, the Unknown*. New York: Harper, 1935.

The First Macrobiotic Cookbook. Oroville, California: George Ohsawa Macrobiotic Foundation, 1986.

Herrigel, Eugen, *Zen in the Art of Archery*. New York: Pantheon, 1953.

Jarvis, D.C., *Folk Medicine*. New York: Holt, 1959.

Kervran, C. Louis, *Transmutations Biologiques*. Paris: Librarie Maloine, S.A., 1962.

Kervran, C. Louis, *Transmutations Naturelles*. Paris: Librarie Maloine, S.A., 1963.

Levy-Bruhl, L., *The "Soul" of the Primitive*. New York: Macmillan, 1928.

Longgood, William, *The Poisons in Your Food*. New York: Simon and Schuster, 1960.

Margine, Dr. S., *Medical Essay and Observation*. Edinburgh: 1747.

Medical Economics. Oradell, N.J.: Medical Economics, Inc., 1923.

New York Times. April 4, 1961, p. 22.

Northrop, F.S.C., *The Meeting of East and West*. New York: Macmillan. 1947.

Ohsawa, Georges, *L'Ere Atomique*. Paris: Vrin, 1962.

Ohsawa, George, *The Philosophy of Oriental Medicine*. Oroville, California: George Ohsawa Macrobiotic Foundation, 1991.

Pascal, Blaise, "Pensees." *Great Books* (Encyclopedia Britannica) Vol. XXXIII, section vi, page 347.

Quinton, Rene, *L'Eau de Mer*. Paris: Masson et Cie., 1912.

Schweitzer, Albert, *Les Grands Penseurs de l'Inde*. Paris: Payot, 1952.

The Manual of Epictetus. Oxford: Clarendon, 1916.

Toynbee, A.J., *A Study of History*. 12 vols., London: Oxford, 1935.

[Note: References to *The Book of Judgment* and *Zen Cookery* in earlier editions have been changed throughout the text to the currently available titles; *The Philosophy of Oriental Medicine* and *The First Macrobiotic Cookbook* respectively. -ed.]

The Author

George Ohsawa (Yukikazu Sakurazawa) was born in Kyoto, the old capital of Japan, on October 18, 1893. He is the author of over three hundred books and papers, ten of which have been published in France since 1926. His best seller is *A New Theory of Nutrition and Its Therapeutic Effect*, written and published in Japan in 1920 and now in its seven-hundredth printing. He has spent thirty years introducing Oriental culture to Europe while simultaneously interpreting the culture of the West for Japan. Among his many translations into Japanese are *Man, the Unknown* by Alexis Carrel and *The Meeting of East and West* by F.S.C. Northrop.

[Those interested in further information on George Ohsawa are encouraged to read *Essential Ohsawa*, which contains a compilation of Ohsawa's writings along with photographs and anecdotes provided by those who knew him best, a chronology of Ohsawa's life, and a complete bibliography of his prodigious writings. Ohsawa died at the age of 73 on April 24, 1966. -ed.]

George Ohsawa — 1893-1966

Books by George Ohsawa

The Art of Peace
(a new translation of *Le Livre du Judo*)

Essential Ohsawa
(edited by Carl Ferré)

Gandhi, the Eternal Youth

Macrobiotics: An Invitation to Health and Happiness
(with Herman Aihara)

Macrobiotics: The Way of Healing
(formerly *Cancer and the Philosophy of the Far East*)

The Order of the Universe

The Philosophy of Oriental Medicine
(formerly *The Book of Judgment*)

The Unique Principle

You Are All Sanpaku
(with William Dufty)

Zen Macrobiotics

A complete selection of macrobiotic books is available from the **George Ohsawa Macrobiotic Foundation**, 1999 Myers Street, Oroville, California 95966; (916) 533-7702.